D1737048

SAMUEL PUFENDORF

JAGIELLONIAN STUDIES IN HISTORY

Editor in chief
Jan Jacek Bruski

Vol. 5

Wojciech Krawczuk

SAMUEL PUFENDORF

AND SOME STORIES OF

THE NORTHERN WAR 1655-1660

Jagiellonian University Press

REVIEWER
Björn Asker

SERIES COVER DESIGN
Jan Jacek Bruski

COVER DESIGN
Agnieszka Winciorek
Front cover: The siege of Cracow, 1655 (Fragment), by Erik Dahlbergh, private collection

This publication was financed by the Jagiellonian University in Krakow – Faculty of History

ISBN 978-83-233-3699-0
ISSN 2299-758X

www.wuj.pl

Jagiellonian University Press
Editorial Offices: Michałowskiego 9/2, 31-126 Kraków
Phone: +48 12 663 23 81, +48 12 663 23 82, Fax: +48 12 663 23 83
Distribution: Phone: +48 12 631 01 97, Fax: +48 12 631 01 98
Cell Phone: + 48 506006 674, e-mail: sprzedaz@wuj.pl
Bank: PEKAO SA, IBAN PL 80 1240 4722 1111 0000 4856 3325

Contents

Preface

Due to the drought in the summer of 2012 water in the Vistula River fell to an extraordinarily low level and parts of the riverbed were exposed. Among a variety of rubbish a group of fine baroque sculptures made of marble emerged; the architectural ornaments, parts of a chiselled fountain, a cartouche with the coat of arms of the Royal House of Vasa. These were remnants of the booty that the Swedes seized in Warsaw in 1656. One of the many, overloaded transport boats sank right after the departure. All subsequent attempts to pick up the heavy sculptures failed. Only after 350 years, a group of scientists from the University of Warsaw managed to unearth this treasure.[1]

The age of the Second Northern War 1655–1660, also called "The Swedish Deluge," still arouses an avid interest in Poland, nor is it forgotten in the neighbouring countries. The North was understood differently, in a broader sense than it is today. Not only did it refer to Scandinavia, but also to Poland, Lithuania and Russia.

The present borders of Sweden, the origins of Prussian militarism, the collapse of the Polish-Lithuanian state and the strengthening of Russia – all these issues can be associated with the said few years, or more specifically, with the time of the war. Thanks to the outstanding novelists, first of all, Henryk Sienkiewicz, the recollection of a heroic struggle became an integral part of the Polish collective memory. Similar memories and legends also exist in other countries: Danes

---

[1] The project began in 2009. Hubert Kowalski and Justyna Jasiewicz, "XVII-wieczne marmury. Skarby z dna Wisły," *Uniwersytet Warszawski. Pismo Uczelni*, no. 56 (February 2012): 30 31, http://portal.uw.edu.pl/c/document_library/get_file?uuid=750ea1a4-72ff-418b-aab3-c9d49a5765ba&groupId=5799051 [7 June 2014].

recall the lost province of Skåne and Swedes the famous crossing over the frozen Belts.

The conflict began in the summer of 1655 with the Swedish attack on the Polish-Lithuanian Commonwealth. Already at that point the contemporaries did not believe that the newly crowned King of Sweden, Charles X Gustav, from the House of Zweibrücken, was so sensitive about the titles and seals – the King of Poland, John Casimir from the House of Vasa, used the title of the King of Sweden after his father King Sigismund.[2] The problem did not concern old dynastic disputes. For Sweden, defined by historians today as a fiscal-military state, the new conflict was the best solution to all the troubles. Charles Gustav was an experienced commander of the Thirty Years War (1618–1648) and had a well trained army at his disposal. The Commonwealth, in turn, was weakened by the long wars with the Cossacks and Moscow, the state was torn by internal conflicts, and powerful magnates were able to effectively block the authority of the King. Since Charles Gustav was supported by the Swedish Council of the Realm, high commanders wanted to take advantage of this situation, even if the Swedish peasants and pastors objected to a new war.

Yet the initial military successes of 1655 proved to be unstable. The great national uprising in Poland and Lithuania seriously weakened the position of the Swedish army. The war spread over larger circles. The Tsar of Russia, The Prince of Transylvania, the Elector of Brandenburg, the Emperor, joined one or the other side. Louis XIV and Oliver Cromwell encouraged Charles Gustav to make military intervention in the Empire. This would mean a further expansion of the conflict on the scale of whole Europe. The King of Sweden, however, chose a different path – in 1657, he abandoned a theatre of war in Poland and attacked Denmark. After a great victory and the ensuing peace treaty in Roskilde in 1658, he decided soon to launch once again the war against the old enemy: Denmark. The titanic struggle ended with the death of Charles Gustav in 1660, which resulted in

---

[2]   Michael Roberts, *The Early Vasas. A History of Sweden, 1523–1611* (Cambridge: Cambridge University Press, 1968), 327–393.

the settlement of the conflict and signing great peace treaties: 1) Sweden with the Commonwealth, Austria and Brandenburg, concluded in Oliva on 3rd May 1660, 2) Sweden with Denmark in Copenhagen, signed on 6th June 1660 and 3) Sweden with Russia, entered into in Kardis on 21st June 1661.

Let us now present the objective, the reservations and the topics of the study. Surely this is not a chronological and systematic description of the events that took place during the Second Northern War. Seven years of the reign of Charles Gustav seethed with bloody battles, daring actions and diplomatic intrigues. These issues are investigated thoroughly and owing to the works of Robert I. Frost the importance of this war is recognized also in the English-language world of the military and diplomatic history.[3] The formulation of a new synthesis would be welcomed, however this would necessitate a large, international team of experts.

The purpose of this study, though, appears to be somewhat different. It was meant as the analysis of selected problems connected with the monumental work of Samuel Pufendorf published under the elaborate title *De rebus a Carolo Gustavo Sveciae Rege, gestis commentariorum libri septem, elegantissimis tabulis aeneis exornati cum triplici indice* (in free translation: *Seven Books on Deeds of Charles Gustav, King of Sweden, adorned with the most elegant illustrations and the triple index*). This immense book, with over 600 pages of the large format *quarto*, was published in 1696 in Nuremberg at the expense of the Swedish state. Within a year it was translated into German and French, and again Sweden covered all the costs.[4] It was but

---

[3] Robert I. Frost, *The Northern Wars. War, State and Society in Northeastern Europe, 1558–1721* (Harlow: Longman, 2000), 156–183; the same author, *After the Deluge: Poland – Lithuania and the Second Northern War* (Cambridge: Cambridge University Press, 1993). See also John Childs, *Warfare in the Seventeenth Century*, Smithsonian History of Warfare (Washington: Smithsonian Books, 2004), 118–121.

[4] Samuel Pufendorf, *Sieben Bücher von denen Thaten Carls Gustavs, Königs in Schweden mit vortrefflichen Kupfern ausgezieret und mit nötigen Registern versehen*, trans. Samuel Rodigast (Nuremberg: Christoph Riegel, 1697); Samuel Pufendorf, *Histoire du Regne de Charles Gustave, Roy de Svede comprise en sept commentaries, enrichis de tailles douces, traduite en francois sur le lutin, de monsieur le baron Samuel de Pufendorf, avec trois indices*, anonymous translation (Nuremberg: Christoph Riegel, 1697). All these works were printed

one of many elements in the long process of creating the aura of the grandeur of the Swedish Kingdom. The unusual efforts of the early modern Swedish authorities with reference to the historiography and antiquarian work are impressive, nonetheless, they served not the science but political purposes in the country and abroad.[5]

Five years I spent translating *Seven books* into Polish serve as the basis and justification of the study undertaken.[6] While juxtaposing the text of Pufendorf with the works of today's historians, I found his message convincing. Unfortunately, except for the military historians, this classic book is rarely used, and even then as a source of interesting details, or, even more frequently, marvellous illustrations. It seems that almost nobody has time to read the book in its entirety. Things do not become easier with the baroque language and the style that today's readers may perceive as tedious. It should be stressed that the presented study is not the language analysis or discussion of the issues related to the translation or terminology – certainly such a project would be very useful, but should embrace all the works of Samuel Pufendorf.

By nature, a translator is forced to read a text many times, to interpret and explain. This, in turn, facilitates recognition of some, not always obvious, intentions of the Author.

Samuel Pufendorf (1632–1694) is most often remembered as a scholar of great renown and achievements in the field of philosophy and the theory of the natural law. His merit as a historian remains in the shade. However, it should be emphasized that during his lifetime it was even this profession that secured his position at courts. In 1677 he was appointed Swedish *Historiographer of the Kingdom*, and after moving to Berlin in 1686 he was given a similar task from the Elec-

---

by the known publisher Christoph Riegel. The Swedish translation by Adolf Hillman, *Sju böcker om konung Carl X Gustafs bragder*, was published in Stockholm only in the years 1912–1915.

[5] Johanna Widenberg, *Fäderneslandets antikviteter. Etniterritoriella historie bruk och integrationssträvanden i den svenska statsmaktens antikvariska verksamhet ca. 1600–1720* (Uppsala: Uppsala Universitet, 2006).

[6] Samuel Pufendorf, *Siedem ksiąg o czynach Karola Gustawa, króla Szwecji*, trans. and ed. by Wojciech Krawczuk (Warszawa: Wydawnictwo DiG, 2013).

tor of Brandenburg.[7] *Seven books* constitute only part of his activity in this field.[8] There is some interest today in this area of Pufendorf's work, to wit the analytical publications of Detlef Döring, Lars Niléhn, and Peter Hanns Reill, yet such undertakings are not too common.[9]

In this respect the research conducted by Arne Stade was and is exceptional. This Swedish historian carried a gigantic, long-term project, and created, *inter alia*, a detailed study on the relationship between the archival collection of Erik Dahlbergh and the research workshop of Samuel Pufendorf.[10] Needless to say, it is possible to resume this work, however, it requires permanent use of the Swedish archives and libraries. Pufendorf benefited from free access to the state archives, which in his time were usually closed to the scientists. Many of the documents he used may not exist today. Stade also drew our attention to the fact, often overlooked, that Samuel Pufendorf was a contemporary and eyewitness to some events of the Second Northern War, his comments are – in part – observations of a participant in this great conflict. He as well had a privilege to meet many distinguished diplomats and commanders of the age.

---

[7] Bo Lindberg, "Samuel Pufendorf," in *Svenskt Biografiskt Lexikon*, vol. 29, ed. Göran Nilzén (Stockholm: 1995–1997), 512–522. Pufendorf's predecessors at the office were called *historians of the King* (historiographus regius), yet he was termed *historian of the Kingdom* (regni historiographus), Bo Bennich-Björkman, *Författaren i ämbetet. Studier i funktion och organization av författarämbeten vid svenska hovet och kansliet 1550-1850* (Uppsala: Svenska bokförlaget, 1970), 211–215.

[8] To name only: Samuel Pufendorf, *Einleitung zu der Historie der vornehmsten Reiche und Staaten* (Frankfurt am Main 1682), or *Commentariorum de rebus Suecicis libri XXVI ab expeditione Gustavi Adolfi Regis in Germaniam ab abdicationem usque Christinae* (Duisburg 1686) and *De rebus gestis Friderici Wilhelmi Magni, electoris Brandenburgici, commentariorum libri novendecim* (Berlin 1695).

[9] Detlef Döring, *Pufendorf Studien: Beiträge zur Biographie Samuel von Pufendorfs und zu seiner Entwicklung als Historiker und theologischer Schriftsteller* (Berlin: Duncker & Humblot, 1992); the same author "Die Privatbibliothek Samuel Pufendorfs," *Zentralblatt für Bibliothekwesen*, vol. 104, part 3 (1990): 102–112; Lars Niléhn, "On the Use of Natural Law. Samuel Pufendorf as Royal Swedish State Historian," in *Skrifter utgivna av Institutet för rättshistorisk forskning. Rättshistoriska Studier*, vol. 12 (Stockholm, 1986): 52–69; Peter Hanns Reill, *The German Enlightenment and the Rise of Historicism* (Berkeley: University of California Press, 1975).

[10] Arne Stade, *Erik Dahlbergh och Carl X Gustafs krigshistoria. Carl Gustaf Studier*, vol. 3 (Kristianstad: Militärhistoriska Förlaget, 1967).

The goals of this study are much narrower than the goals Stade set. First of all, I would like to consider how Samuel Pufendorf presents the past, and whether his storytelling is unique. It is as well worth asking whether the Author could and tried to objectively describe the very dramatic events of the Charles Gustav's rule, or, as some say, whether he was only a panegyrist extolling the glorious reign of the dynasty of Pfalz–Zweibrücken, and finally, what methods he used to construct "objective" history.

Many issues addressed in *Seven books* are still being debated. When translating the said work, I wanted initially to prepare a kind of synthesis on the latest research on Pufendorf's *Seven books*. Nonetheless, it quickly proved impossible, for the bibliography *Poland during the Second Northern War 1655–1660*, published in 1957, comprises 2,440 positions, and for the last half a century many valuable studies have been added to the list.[11]

However, in the text submitted below, I have tried to return to this original intention. It would be good to invite Samuel Pufendorf to a panel discussion on the Second Northern War. Since it is unfeasible, I decided to introduce a substantial number of quotations from his work, juxtaposing them with the statements of other historians. Because of my limited experience, the topics raised concern more often the Polish-Lithuanian Commonwealth than other states described in *Seven books*. I attempted to find such issues that continue to arouse emotions or are presented in various ways, depending on the historiographical traditions of the given country.

All the English translations, unless stated otherwise, are mine, they are presented with the abbreviation: trans. W.K. When it comes to the geographical names, the English names were preferred, so in the main text it is *Warsaw*, not *Warszawa*, however not always, so there is also *Gdańsk* not *Danzig*, and in such cases, the other, i.e. English/German, form is given in parentheses at the first occurrence of the name.

---

[11] Adam Przyboś, ed., *Polska w okresie drugiej wojny północnej 1655–1660*, vol. 3 (Warszawa: Państwowe Wydawnictwo Naukowe, 1957).

All the dates encountered in the work of Pufendorf are consistent with the Julian calendar (Old Style). Protestant Sweden adopted the Gregorian calendar (New Style) only in 1753. But in Catholic countries, such as the Archduchy of Austria, France or Poland-Lithuania, the New Style calendar was in use already from 1582. Thus, in historical sources and publications one and the same event can be dated variously depending on the writers preferences. By way of illustration, to converse the date of the Julian calendar to the Gregorian one for the years of the Second Northern War, we must add ten to the first date, remembering about leap years in 1656 and 1660.

The shortcuts *De rebus* and less frequently *Seven books* denominate the analyzed work of Samuel Pufendorf, i.e. the aforementioned *De rebus a Carolo Gustavo Sveciae Rege, gestis commentariorum libri septem, elegantissimis tabulis aeneis exornati cum triplici indice.* I used the first original Latin edition – Nuremberg 1696 – which is easily available online, as well as the German and French translations.

Acknowledgements

While working on this project, I benefitted greatly from the help of my colleagues from the Institute of History of the Jagiellonian University. I would like to express my gratitude to everyone, and especially to the Director of the Institute, Professor Sławomir Sprawski, Vice-Director, Professor Stanisław Pijaj and to the Editor of the English Book Series, Professor Jan Jacek Bruski. I would also like to thank my Publisher, Jagiellonian University Press, for the assistance they offered.

I am indebted to the Director Hubert Wajs and Vice-Director Jacek Krochmal from the Central Archives of Historical Records in Warsaw (Archiwum Główne Akt Dawnych), who repeatedly invited me to the *Baltic Colloquium* held regularly at this institution. It was a unique opportunity to discuss many theses of this book in a very friendly atmosphere.

For many references and advice I am especially grateful to Professor Björn Asker and Dr Jonas Nordin.

I was privileged to enjoy the cooperation with the expert proofreaders: Joanna Szczepańska-Włoch and Małgorzata Szul, who corrected the whole text, and Justyna Fenrych, who helped with Chapter I. I would also like to thank Jadwiga Makowiec, the technical editor, for her help.

Last but not least, I would like to extend a personal thank to my family: Parents, Wife Agnieszka and Daughter Marysia for their understanding and support.

Chapter I: A sense of time

What if time flows not, if its progress is only a kind of illusion? There is a possibility that our perception of past and future is wrong, that only presence exists.[1] For any historian the notion of time should be crucial, but quite often we forget about the implications and fallacies that arise from our comprehension of this phenomenon. The most common attitude the researchers cultivate is linked to the feeling of omnipotence and omniscience, which they show in their studies. How often is it that we encounter acerbic remarks on certain commands, battle plans or diplomatic missions? "It should not have been done," exclaims the demigod scholar, "why, everyone could see that this was a mistake! How could such a stupid scheme be adopted?" It is quite an easy task to criticize past generations for not seeing clearly what would happen.[2] The irritating habit of scholars to express their superiority about past events is of the same value as stock brokers predictions concerning share prices. Fortunately, there is no stock exchange for the opinions of historians.

In his thorough book on German historiography in the age of Enlightenment, Peter Hanns Reill presented a typology of Samuel Pufendorf's historical works and noted his specific understanding of the matter of time. Following Georges Gurvitch's terminology, Reill describes it as "erratic," where "the present appears to prevail over the past and the future," and no historical development seems to take place. The method used by Pufendorf is most often a simple descrip-

---

[1]   Paul Davies, "That Mysterious Flow," *Scientific American* 287 (September 2002): 40–47.
[2]   See the remarks of Wiesław Majewski, "Sienkiewicz – przodek nas, historyków," in *Epoka Ogniem i mieczem we współczesnych badaniach historycznych. Zbiór studiów*, ed. Mirosław Nagielski (Warszawa: Wydawnictwo DiG, 2000), 99.

tion of events – these are modern chronicles, in which stories are disconnected, are presented as separate, closed entities. According to Pufendorf, the truth from the past can be useful, but it is the analysis of the contemporary events that is especially valuable. The science of history is therefore merely "auxiliary to political science."[3] Basically, Reill's description has to be accepted. There is, then, one point which should be discussed – are there any positive aspects of such an understanding of time and "eternization of the present"?

The fortress

Even to this day the fortress of Jasna Góra (*Mount Luminous*) in Częstochowa has not lost much of its martial appearance. It envelops and protects only the cloister of the Holy Mary and few adjacent buildings, but the decision to raise huge bastions around the shrine was not taken by the ecclesiastical dignitaries, but by King Sigismund III Vasa in the year 1620.[4] At this time it was probably regarded as a link in the chain of fortresses which defended the western border of the Polish-Lithuanian Commonwealth in the restless age of the Thirty Years' War. Fortunately, even when the neighbouring country of Silesia was disturbed and much destroyed during this prolonged conflict, the small fortress of Jasna Góra never came under siege. The Commonwealth remained neutral and the fortified cloister waited more than thirty years before its baptism of fire. A great treasure of all the Polish Catholics rested inside the monastery – the icon of Our Lady of Częstochowa, known also as the Black Madonna, worshipped to this day as the Protectress of Poland.

---

[3] Peter Hanns Reill, *The German Enlightenment and the Rise of Historicism* (Berkeley: University of California Press, 1975), 16–21. Reill thoroughly discusses different types of Pufendorf's historical works but is rather sceptical of the evaluation – there is "no inner coherence, no linkage of events he (Pufendorf) described."

[4] Bogusław Dybaś, *Fortece Rzeczypospolitej. Studium z dziejów budowy fortyfikacji stałych w państwie polsko-litewskim w XVII wieku* (Toruń: Towarzystwo Naukowe w Toruniu, 1998), 186.

The external works were designed in accordance with the guide-lines of the Old Dutch School of Fortification, very popular in Poland and Lithuania at the time.[5] There were four major bastions in the four corners of the *Fortalitium Marianum*, each of them equipped with two chambers – the lower for artillery and the upper for musketry. Only one of the original bastions, bearing the name of Saint Roch, is preserved and gives us an idea of the whole structure.

John Casimir Vasa, King of Poland, often visited the famous cloister. He did so in 1654 as well, when the Commonwealth faced invasion from the east – from Muscovy. Yet this journey did not win admiration of the, usually pious, Polish elite. The echo of discontent reached Pufendorf even many years later, who – always suspicious of the Catholic rites – noted that "although the Polish states asked, and it had been recently decided at the Diet that the king should immediately proceed to Lithuania, where the greatest threat from the enemy was, John Casimir shied it away under various guises, either because of pilgrimages to Częstochowa, Kalwaria and other places, or because of appointed court sessions."[6]

The siege

The threat to the monastery came when the campaign of 1655 already finished and almost the whole Kingdom of Poland was subjugated by the Swedes. John Casimir fled the country. The victory seemed complete. Nevertheless, the Swedish army had to be dispersed into smaller units, which were sent off to different regions to collect taxes and maintain order. Charles X Gustav tried to impose harsh discipline on his soldiers – many were hanged in the first weeks

[5]   Janusz Bogdanowski, *Sztuka obronna* (Kraków: Zarząd Jurajskich Parków Krajobrazowych, 1993), 60–61.

[6]   Samuel Pufendorf, *De rebus a Carolo Gustavo Sveciae Rege, gestis commentariorum libri septem, elegantissimis tabulis aeneis exornati cum triplici indice* (Nuremberg 1696), 1: § 49 (trans. Wojciech Krawczuk).

of the war because of small offenses – but looting was a natural habit for hardened veterans of the Thirty Years' War. It was already in August that the Swedish king had to instantly remind his officers about their duty to maintain order in the ranks.[7] In the autumn, after many victories, the time of harvest came and the army had to sustain itself through enforced contributions. The fact that most soldiers in the Swedish ranks were German Protestants did not help in their contact with Catholic Poles. The population began to stir, which resulted in insignificant clashes between loosely organized groups of insurgents, which consisted of Polish nobility and peasants. Częstochowa and its cloister were in the vicinity of the troubled region of Wielkopolska.

A decision to force Jasna Góra to surrender was reached by the local Swedish commander, General Lieutenant Burchard Müller, on 18th November 1655.[8] Charles X Gustav was not particularly content with such an action, since it could damage relations with the Catholics and cause further trouble. The monks of St. Paul, inhabitants of the place, had already obtained a letter of protection from the Swedish Field Marshall Arvid Wittenberg. They submitted to Charles Gustav, as almost everyone in Poland in 1655. Yet they knew perfectly well that letters and promises would not guard them against acts of violence and that Swedes would occupy the fortress owing to its strategic importance. The monks feared the Protestants and did not want to let them into the monastery. In the last moment of peace the icon of Black Madonna was hidden in the castle of Lubliniec, across the Silesian border.

The great advantage of the besieged was their leader, the prior – father Augustyn Kordecki. Although he did not possess any military or diplomatic experience, he still dominated over the foe in both these aspects. The cloister was also well equipped with some heavy artillery

---

[7]   Lars Tersmeden, "Carl X Gustafs armé. En konturteckning mot bakgrund av kriget mot Polen," in *Carl X Gustafs armé. Carl – Gustaf-Studier*, vol. 8, ed. Arne Stade, (Kristianstad: Militärhistoriska Förlaget, 1979), 37–39.

[8]   The best up-to-date description of the siege is to be found in the article by Zbigniew Wójcik, "Tło historyczne obrony Klasztoru Jasnogórskiego w roku 1655," in: *Częstochowa. Dzieje miasta i Klasztoru Jasnogórskiego*, vol. 1: *Okres staropolski*, ed. Feliks Kiryk (Częstochowa: Urząd Miasta Częstochowa, 2002), 303–35.

and a supply of gunpowder. There was a squad of musketeers brought in from Wrocław (*Breslau*) in Silesia so the whole garrison amounted to c. 240 soldiers, there were as well many refugees inside who could lend a hand. We do not know the exact number of the Swedish forces, but there were markedly fewer soldiers than 9,000 – this number is generally rejected as incredible.[9]

Kordecki refused to open the gates even at the request of Müller. However, to soften such a rebuff, he stated that the monks were loyal subjects to the Swedish king. Anyway, during the whole siege negotiations were as intense as military actions. There was one main point the monks would not yield to – no heretic soldier was to enter the cloister. They could have already known about the atrocities against Catholic priests and monks perpetrated by the Swedish army – like in the town of Kazimierz near Kraków, where Canons Regular from the parish church of Corpus Christi were oppressed by raving and drunk soldiers.[10]

Kordecki did not openly reject demands from the Swedish side, but stressed that Müller's mandate concerned the occupation of the nearby town of Częstochowa, not the cloister of Jasna Góra, which did not belong to the town. Such arguments could only prolong the negotiations. A formal siege began after the cease-fire expired, on November 21st.

The attacking forces were unprepared for such actions, as they only had light field guns, hence the bombardment was not exceedingly dangerous at the beginning. In turn, solid rock under the fortress made it difficult to dig trenches. The Polish garrison managed to arrange some successful outings, consequently, the spirits on the Polish side revived. Regrettably, though, the crisis erupted after a few days. Some Polish soldiers and nobles wanted to surrender, at which point Kordecki did not falter and expelled the leaders of mutiny from Jasna Góra.

---

[9] Adam Kersten, *Pierwszy opis obrony Jasnej Góry w 1655 r.* (Warszawa: Książka i Wiedza, 1959), 103.

[10] Stefan Ranotowicz, *Opisanie inkursji Szwedów do Polski do Krakowa (1655–1657)*, ed. Józef Mitkowski (Kraków: Towarzystwo Miłośników i Zabytków Krakowa, 1958), 15.

But even on the Swedish side the situation was far from joyful. Admittedly, Müller received new reinforcements and a few pieces of heavy artillery, yet the firing from the monastery was accurate and the losses were high. Swedes were also low on gunpowder. On 14th December gunners from Jasna Góra destroyed one of the two heaviest Swedish cannons – the 24 pounder. Even the arrival of supplies for Swedes, on the night of 23rd December, did not alter their general feeling of defeat.

After issuing final demands, Müller decided to end the siege, and retreated on the night of 26th December 1655. The first news announcing the successful defence of Jasna Góra cloister began to spread around the country. Such an opportunity to incite the rebellion against the Swedes could not be missed by the exiled Polish king, let alone the Polish queen.

The legend

The Swedish failure at Jasna Góra was not important from a strategic point of view. There is, however, a controversy, still unresolved by the Polish historians, specifically, did the siege and Polish victory give an incentive to the popular uprising against the Swedes in the whole country? Or maybe the importance of this success was only highlighted in the following years, to raise fighting spirits of masses and to change the war into a religious conflict?

Already in November 1655 the Polish court, staying in exile in Silesia, attempted to begin a propaganda campaign in which the Swedish invasion was presented as a religious conflict.

> Meanwhile, John Casimir in Silesia, where he escaped, worked hard on regaining trust of Poles and obtaining help from all sides. The severity of fate caused that the resentment of his subjects turned at once into compassion among many. [...] John Casimir sent letters from Opole to all the Polish states as well, in which he freed himself from the blame for all the misfortunes that had hit Poland so far. He presented the state of misery of the time and called for the restoration of ancestral religion and freedom. He also promised to forget what had happened, threaten-

ing that those who would not follow him to the letter and would still stay with the Swedes would be guilty of treason. The mood of the people darkened owing to the tales of the priests who were worried about the Roman rites and who talked about the Swedes in deep hatred, for they looted some churches where many inhabitants of the provinces protected their belongings.[11]

The idea to record the siege of Jasna Góra for posterity and to use it in warfare propaganda emerged for the first time in December 1655 – when the struggle was not yet concluded. It was the Polish Queen Louise Marie Gonzaga who expressed such an intention in conversation with one of the monks of Jasna Góra in Silesia. The queen was a cunning politician, though, her activity was severely restricted in the age dominated by men.

It was not only domestic recipients of this message who should be acquainted with the miraculous defence of the holy shrine. By order of the Queen, her secretary, Pierre de Noyers, kept especially French public opinion informed about the recent events in Poland. The stakes were high – Louis XIV could influence his Swedish ally, cut financial aid and enforce negotiations. The religious dimension of the struggle in Poland was as well of uttermost importance. The arch-Catholic King of France could support Sweden in a dynastic quarrel with the Polish Vasas, but not in the religious conflict. The Queen's efforts bore fruit, *Gazette de France* described the siege of Jasna Góra.[12] Even Pufendorf records that situation in the *Seven books*, although he did not know about the exact cause of the problems in France:

It seemed that the French were most worried that damage would be inflicted on the Catholic Church in Poland. Notices with the appeal hung on the corner of each street in Paris: if Poland gets no aid, the Catholic religion will fall there. The king of France himself recommended Charles Gustav, through [the French envoy] d'Avaugour, to take care of the clergy and places of worship.

In the time of the Thirty Years' War his father [Louis XIII] obliged Gustavus Adolphus and Christina to fulfil his wish, for it was the best way to conciliate the followers of different denominations. When Louis XIV heard that Charles Gustav did not intend to make any changes to the religion in Poland, he expressed his appreciation.[13]

---

[11] Pufendorf, *De rebus*, 2: § 70.

[12] Kersten, *Pierwszy opis*, 293–294.

[13] Pufendorf, *De rebus*, 2: § 93, trans. W.K.

Still the main undertaking – a broad description of the siege – had to be provided. It was the prior Kordecki who completed this important work, in the second half of 1656.[14] The book was printed in Cracow, probably at the end of 1657, under the long title *Nova Gigantomachia Contra Sacram Imaginem Deiparae Virginis a Sancto Luca depictam, Et in Monte Claro Częstochouiensi Apud Religiosos Patres Ordinis S. Pauli Primi Eremitae, in celeberrimo Regni Poloniae Coenebio collocatam, Per Suecos et alios Haereticos excitata, Et Ad perpetuam beneficiorem Gloriosae Deiparae Virginis recordationem, successurae posteritati fideliter conscripta A R.P. Fr. Avgvstino Kordecki praedicti Ordinis, protunc Clari Montis Priore. Anno Domini M.DC.LV.*

Kordecki's account was the main source for the historians writing about the siege to the end of the 19th century. The prior, however, omitted some thorny questions – like the verbal (not factual) surrender of the cloister to the rule of Charles Gustav. In the 20th century, in turn, after a period of uncritical admiration, his work, at which grave and often unjust charges were levelled, was rejected. It is to the great merit of Adam Kersten who in the already cited book, conducted a thorough analysis of *Nova Gigantomachia* and separated the wheat from the chaff.

Despite all the criticism, Kordecki's view on the siege prevails among the Polish public today, owing to a historian, Ludwik Kubala, and a novelist, Henryk Sienkiewicz. In his exhaustive book, *Swedish War in the Years 1655–1656*, Kubala convincingly linked the narrative of *Nova Gigantomachia* to other sources.[15] Availing himself of the Kubala's research, Sienkiewicz, in turn, succeeded in revitalizing the old legend in his novel *The Deluge (Potop)*, printed in the years

---

[14] Kersten, *Pierwszy opis*, 39. Częstochowa was the very place where in March 1657 King John Casimir organized an important convention of senators and nobles, at which they prepared strategic plans for further actions. Robert I. Frost, *After the Deluge. Poland – Lithuania and the Second Northern War 1655–1660* (Cambridge: Cambridge University Press, 1993), 87–92; Adam Kersten, *Stefan Czarniecki 1599–1665* (Warszawa: Wydawnictwo Ministerstwa Obrony Narodowej, 1963), 333–36.

[15] Ludwik Kubala, *Wojna szwecka w roku 1655 i 1656* (Lwów: Biblioteka Historyczna Altenberga, 1880), one of the four volumes on the Second Northern War 1655–1660.

1884–1886. The strength of *Deluge*, however, lies in excellent style and dynamic structure of the plot.[16]

A fictional character in *Deluge*, a famous soldier and brawler Andrzej Kmicic arrives at the monastery to warn the monks of the impending Swedish attack. He uses the false name of Babinicz, because he betrayed the Polish king while serving the Lithuanian field commander Janusz Radziwiłł, who secretly surrendered to Charles Gustav. Now Kmicic wants to make amends, to be absolved of all the blame. He bravely fights on the walls of the cloister and in a solitary escapade destroys a great Swedish culverin – the 24 pounder.[17]

Sienkiewicz did not describe any miraculous deeds, therefore, such an approach made the story credible. Still, there are some hints which must have touched the audience and justified the Polish-Catholic case. When the Swedes began to dig a mine under the cloister, the mood of those besieged broke. But at that very moment:

> A wonderful sign was made manifest. Behold all about them all of a sudden the sound of wings was heard, and flocks of small winter birds appeared in the court of the fortress, and all the time new ones flew in from the starved countryside around. Birds such as gray larks, ortolans, buntings with yellow breasts, poor sparrows, green titmice, red bulfinches, sat on the slopes of the roofs, on the quoins, on the jambs, on the church cornices. Other flew around forming a colourful crown above the head of the prior, flapping their wings, chirping sadly as if begging for alms, and having no fear whatsoever of man. The people present were amazed at the sight, and Kordecki, after he had prayed for a while, said at last:
> See these little birds of the forest. They come to protect the Mother of God, but you doubt Her power.[18]

There could be no mistake that the divine powers were benevolent and supportive. The calm firmness of the besieged manifested itself also in the most joyful of all the Catholic feasts:

---

[16] It was also Adam Kersten who traced the links between Sienkiewicz's *Deluge* and *Nova Gigantomachia* in the book *Sienkiewicz – Potop – historia* (Warszawa: Państwowy Instytut Wydawniczy, 1974), 171–91.

[17] Henryk Sienkiewicz's *Deluge* was translated in 1891 into English by Jeremiah Curtin and published in Boston at Little, Brown and company, 1915. It is available online and I used this version making some alterations. There is, however, a very good modern translation by Wiesław S. Kuniczak.

[18] Sienkiewicz, *Deluge*, trans. J. Curtin, 2: 92, with some alterations by W.K.

At last Christmas Eve came. With the first star, great and small lights began to shine all around in the fortress. The night was still, frosty, but clear. The Swedish soldiers, stiffened with cold in the entrenchments, gazed from below on the dark walls of the unapproachable fortress and to their minds came the warm Scandinavian cottages stuffed with moss, their wives and children, the fir-tree gleaming with lights; and more than one iron breast swelled with a sigh, with regret, with homesickness, with despair. But in the fortress, at tables covered with hay, the besieged were breaking Christmas wafers. A quiet joy was shining in everyone's faces, for each one had the premonition, almost the certitude, that the hours of suffering would be soon at an end.[19]

The combined forces of Kordecki's and Sienkiewicz's persuasive talents convinced even the communist leaders of People's Republic of Poland. Without any hesitation, they funded the film adaptation of *Deluge*, screened in the cinemas in 1974. The climax of this Oscar-nominated movie is of course the successful defence of Jasna Góra. It seems that every generation explains the story about the last stand of the Black Madonna monastery anew. Hence it has become an unshakable part of Polish historical memory.

Pufendorf's tale

We shall, however, check at last how Pufendorf describes the siege. He notes it in the Second Book of *De rebus* in paragraph 36 which bears the title *Svecorum exigua damna*, also *Irrelevant Losses of the Swedes*. In Pufendorf's account Landgraf von Hessen-Eschwege was killed in an ambush by the town of Kościan on 25th September 1655, and to avenge his death and to disperse the rebels, Charles Gustav sent a disciplining force under the command of Count Wrzesowicz. Those refusing to obey the Swedish orders were called rebels for the fact that the nobility of the province of Wielkopolska (Greater Poland) swore allegiance to the king of Sweden in Ujście at the very beginning of war. Nonetheless, it did not protect Wielkopolska from problems.

---

[19] Sienkiewicz, *Deluge*, 2: 94.

The said events draw us near Jasna Góra, ergo it appears to be justified to quote Pufendorf's view on the matter:

> Paulo post quoque octingenti circiter Nobiles Poloni conglobati praefectum turmae ad tributa exigenda missum non procul Fravenstadio cum quadraginta equitibus interceptum, fustibusque contusum capite truncaverant. His coercendis Rex Burchardum Müllerum Wresovicio junctum majoris Poloniae curam agere jussit, ac conglobatos rebelles dissipare, quos inveniret cedere ac latibula eorum destruere.

There were also c. eight hundred Polish nobles, who formed a party and attacked one Swedish captain with forty cavalrymen. The Swedes were sent to collect taxes in the province of Wielkopolska. In the vicinity of the town of Wschowa (Fraustadt) the officer was detained by the rebellious Poles, flogged and decapitated. To disrupt such offences, Charles Gustav decided to send Burchard Müller as aid to Wrzesowicz. Both had to take care of Wielkopolska, disperse the rebels, kill any who could be found and destroy their hideouts (Today such an action would probably be defined as peace-keeping or anti-terrorism procedures). No siege was planned, but it was clear that all the fortified places should remain in Swedish possession. Some doubts were raised in the Swedish headquarters as to the cruelty of Wrzesowicz, that perhaps it was counterproductive, and that his actions had the effect of infuriating rather than pacifying the population.

There are only two sentences concerning the siege of Jasna Góra:

> Ast Müllerus Czenstochoviam munitum coenobium in potestatem redigere cupidus, cum monachos persuoasionibus movere non posset, ut praesidium reciperent, vim adhibere constituit, petitis Cracovia duabus machinis majoribus. Sed vim admovere vetuit Rex, ne hiberno obsidio copiae atterentur, neu populus superstitione loci imbutus eo facto offenderetur.

In the light of the already quoted studies we can agree with the first sentence: "but Müller wanted to subdue the fortified cloister of Częstochowa and when he could not persuade the monks to accept the [Swedish] garrison, he decided to take the monastery by force and demanded two big cannons from Cracow." It was Müller's decision to attack the cloister, Charles Gustav and his generals wavered in that matter. Yet the second sentence is partly wrong: "The King prohibited the use of force both to avoid destroying his troops by the winter siege and offending the population filled with superstitions concerning this place." Pufendorf stresses here that the king forbade the use of force – which is untrue. We know that Charles Gustav demanded lenient treatment of the cloister, and Müller acted somewhat out of his orders. The siege was long and violent, however, negotiations were conducted continuously and were as intense as the fight itself. The Swedish king ordered the end of the assault, but there was one condition to be completed by the monks: they had to swear a new oath of submission to Charles Gustav. A vow of silence on the matter allows us to assume that they did not surrender. Despite all the criticism directed at Pufendorf for such a short and minimalist description of the siege, his account is essentially true. But it does not have much to do with the legend of Jasna Góra's defence, which was established later.

We have to return here to our reflections on the sense of time. In December 1655 the siege was a minor nuisance for the Swedish forces, after an overwhelming victory in the great campaign. It was just the irrelevant opposition to be crushed. Maybe some of the high-ranking generals or the king himself had a sense of foreboding of further complications with Jasna Góra – but nothing more. There were similar problems with rebels in Piotrków, Nowy Sącz, Łęczyca and many other places. The picture of events in Pufendorf's work is probably the same as the Swedish generals perceived it in that very moment. The future was unknown.

But was the depiction of the struggle carefully thought out by the *Historiographer Royal* when he wrote his account tens of years later? Arne Stade raised a similar question relating to Pufendorf's method of work with respect to his use of Erik Dahlberg's papers concerning the famous crossing of the Belt straits in 1658.[20] Stade pointed out that Pufendorf had at his disposal a large number of sources – both printed and unpublished. He preferred the former, but even then he

---

[20] Arne Stade, "Erik Dahlbergh och Carl X Gustafs krigshistoria," in *Carl X Gustaf-Studier*, vol. 3, ed. Arne Stade (Kristianstad: Militärhistoriska Förlaget, 1967), 299–300.

did not have enough time to analyze, to "digest" such mass of documents. In the case of Jasna Góra, Pufendorf had to be content with manuscripts, most probably letters written at the time of the siege. He produced an effect, which was most probably unintended – a kind of suspense, in which the knowledge acquired later did not interfere with the description of events that were shown in the contemporary environment.

If we want to know about the origins of the legend of the Jasna Góra siege, unquestionably, Kordecki and Sienkiewicz should act as our guides. But if we prefer to learn what the siege disclosed for the spectators and participants in that theatre of war at the end of 1655 and the beginning of 1656, we should rather start our investigations with a few sentences from the Pufendorf's work. Therefore, Adam Kersten's remark requires our attention: "Pufendorf's *De rebus* is the only known foreign [i.e. non-Polish – W.K.] historiographical work of the 17ᵗʰ century, in which the case of Jasna Góra was listed."[21]

---

[21] Kersten, *Pierwszy opis*, 298.

Chapter II: Judging the deeds

And so we proceed to the deeds of Charles Gustav, which should be properly investigated, described and judged.[1] The new philosophy of evaluating the political matters comes in *De rebus* to the foreground. The role of God, so important in the mediaeval order of things, at the end of the 17th century was diffused and expressed more subtly. Samuel Pufendorf, representing a new system of thought, based on the reinterpreted law of nature, stressed the importance of the social contract as the foundation for the society. Unquestionably, the King himself should be the keystone of such a structure granted that the monarch exercised absolute power. Loose forms of the social contract, such as the *forma mixta* in the Polish-Lithuanian Commonwealth or in the Holy Roman Empire of the German Nation, earned a sharp rebuke from the Philosopher.[2]

In *De rebus* Pufendorf scarcely recalls the God (*Deus*), or Providence (*Providentia*). The last notion was understood at this age as the God's plan for the world. These terms can be found in *Seven books*, but they are most often presented as quotes from diplomatic acts, or inscriptions on medals, commemorative coins, engravings, etc. Much often will we be faced with the notion of *fatum*. Andreas Hellerstedt, who studied understanding of this concept in the early-18th-century

---

[1]   For a modern biography of Charles Gustav, see Björn Asker, *Karl X Gustav* (Lund: Historiska Media, 2010).

[2]   Factually, the critique of the empire Pufendorf presented was so acute that he printed it under the pseudonym Severinus de Monzambano, fearing consequences. Samuel Pufendorf, *The Present State of Germany*, trans. Edmund Bohun, ed. Michael J. Seidler (Indianapolis: Liberty Fund, 2007).

Sweden, explains *fatum* as "chain of natural forces."[3] And it was obviously much more to the Pufendorf's liking. Finally, not a Christian, but pagan idea of *Fortuna* – appears also in *De rebus* construed as luck which unexpectedly could spoil or destroy someone, randomly and without clear fault.

Deprived (at least partially) of the godly empowerment, the King had to confirm his authority. The legitimacy of his rule had to be constructed in an elaborated process, where different means and ways had to be implemented. We know a lot about various methods used in this early modern age, to wit classic work of Peter Burke *The Fabrication of Louis XIV*.[4] The deeds of the monarch, presented in a scientific and objective way, had also to legitimize his claims to the throne. As proved by the study of Anna Maria Forssberg, Charles X Gustav was a great expert in the field of influencing the public opinion in his Kingdom, in this aspect he was a worthy successor to Gustav Vasa and Charles IX.[5]

The "case" of Charles Gustav was, however, additionally delayed by circumstances of his accession to the throne. He was not the hereditary heir to Sweden, and owed the crown to the goodwill of Queen Christina, who abdicated in his favour in 1654. Thanks to his mother – Catharine of Sweden, daughter of King Charles IX – the blood of Vasa's flowed in his veins. But there were many influential opponents of the new dynasty of Pfalz-Zweibrücken at the Swedish court.

In c. 1681, when Pufendorf began his work on *De rebus*, Charles X Gustav had long since been dead. His son, Charles XI, was already introducing the absolute system of government in Sweden. As a result of this action, the political and financial power of aristocracy was crushed, mainly through the process of *reduktionen* – the fiefs granted to nobility were returned to the Crown. The allotment sys-

---

3   Andreas Hellerstedt, *Ödets teater. Ödesföreställningar i Sverige vid 17–hundra talets början* (Lund: Nordic Academic Press, 2009), 80, 106, 203.

4   Peter Burke, *The Fabrication of Louis XIV* (New Haven and London: Yale University Press, 1992).

5   Anna Maria Forssberg, "Att hålla folket på gott humor. Informationsspridning, krigspropaganda och mobilisering i Sverige 1655–1680," *Acta Universitatis Stockholmiensis. Stockholm Studies in History*, vol. 80 (2005).

tem for the army – *indelningsverket* – was completely revised. A small defeat at Fehrbellin in 1675, inflated by the Prussian propaganda, did not change the fact that Sweden was still a great power in the Baltic area. But the dynasty had to be strengthened – also via the historical record of the founder of the new House of Sweden.

Did Charles X Gustav, warmonger and warlord, suit Pufendorf's taste well? Possibly. – Or this reign was not an abstract and far away subject for the *Historiographer Royal*. In 1658 Pufendorf became a tutor of Peter Julius Coyet's children, a Swedish diplomat working in Copenhagen at that time. After the outbreak of the second war with Denmark, the whole household of Coyet was arrested by the Danish authorities. Pufendorf spent eight long months in Danish prison, consequently the memory of this period could affect his perception.[6]

We should, however, give voice to Pufendorf himself. In the first chapter of *De rebus* he declared: "I could promise indeed that this book will be great, if only I had enough wisdom and rhetorical skills to match the magnitude of the matters. Yet, they [the skills] are less than moderate, therefore there is only one reason why I expect a favour for my description with reasonable people: it faithfully reflected unadulterated documents, and was prepared without passion or preconceived opinion."[7] But could he fulfil this promise?

Another Lion of the North?

There was one point where Pufendorf and Swedish policymakers could easily agree on and it concerned the situation in the Empire in

---

[6] Bo Lindberg, "Samuel von Pufendorf," in *Svenskt Biografiskt Lexikon*, ed. Göran Nilzén, vol. 29 (Stockholm 1995–1997), 512–522.

[7] "Quam sane egregiam polliceri possem, si magnitudinem rerum ingenio, dicendique artibus aequare liceret. Sed cum hae infra mediocritatem sint, apud cordatos ex hoc uno commendationem scriptioni meae expecto, quod eadem sincera fide ex indubiis documentis deprompta est, nullo affect aut prejudico interpolate." Pufendorf, *De rebus a Carolo Gustavo Sveciae Rege, gestis commentariorum libri septem, elegantissimis tabulis aeneis exornati cum triplici indice* (Nuremberg 1696), 1: § 1, trans. W.K.

the 1650s. It was far from satisfactory, both for Protestant states and for many Catholic rulers. Since the Treaty of Westphalia, concluded in 1648, Sweden was both a warrantor of its fulfillment and a member of the Holy Roman Empire – because of newly acquired possessions of Principality of Bremen and town of Wismar in the Lower Saxon Circle (*Reichskreis*), Western Pomerania (*Vorpommern*) in Upper Saxon Circle and secularized bishopric of Verden, since 1648 the Principality, in the Lower Rheinish–Westphalian Circle. Until 1650 Charles Gustav represented Sweden at the executive congress in Nuremberg, where the postwar pacification of the empire had to be prepared and implemented. However, his bold plans to arm the states of the Empire and to expel the Spaniards by force were not accepted – nonetheless, the future King made a name for himself.[8]

Michael Seidler in his study on Pufendorf's moral and political philosophy emphasized the efforts of the philosopher to prevent the "destructive social conflict" and war in Germany, where the situation was still explosive at the end of the 17th century.[9] But who was to be blamed for this serious plight? The official Swedish position, formulated in the diplomatic instructions and quoted extensively by Pufendorf, is to be found in *De rebus*, in the *Second Book*, § 41 and 42. The Swedish reasoning and description of the situation was as follows:

Ferdinand III Habsburg died on 2nd April 1657 and the Swedish side had to be prepared for the election of the new emperor. The Habsburgs promoted their kin, Leopold, king of Hungary and second son of late emperor, as his successor. Nothing could be less pleasing for Sweden, however, chances of a Protestant candidate were slim. "It was not about the elevation of any Protestant to the dignity [of emperor], which would force all papists to join forces, but that someone else from their group [of Catholic princes] assumed the imperial diadem. [...] A future emperor should be obliged by an appropriate

---

[8]   Sven Ingemar Olofsson, *Efter Westfaliska Freden. Sveriges yttre politik 1650–1654* (Stockholm: Kungl. Vitterhets Historie och Antikvitets Akademiska Handlingar, 1957), 30–31.

[9]   Michael Seidler, "Pufendorf's Moral and Political Philosophy," in *The Stanford Encyclopedia of Philosophy* (Spring 2013 Edition), ed. Edward N. Zalta, http://plato.stanford.edu/archives/spr2013/entries/pufendorf-moral/ [4 June 2014].

election agreement (*Wahlkapitulation*), which would guarantee the decisions of the Westphalia Treaty and assure that the states [of the Empire] should pay compensation to the allied Kings [of Sweden and France], so that they would not be forced to seek other securities at their discretion." And there was one dynasty responsible for all these troubles. "The intentions of Ferdinand II and III we remember well – how much evil Germany suffered because of immoderate greed of this House [of Habsburg]. How many excuses they made to take up arms and to stir the members of the Empire, how difficult it was to win freedom again – and it would not happen, if the foreign monarchs did not lend a hand."[10] And in the next chapter: "if [Charles Gustav] would be silent now, the states of Germany would lose heart. [...] The electors would have to join the Austrian faction."[11]

Among the European elite a vivid memory of late Gustav II Adolf existed, the "Lion of the North," who in the time of war, helped the Protestants' cause. When in 1656 the Swedish envoy, Christer Bonde, discussed the future cooperation between England and Sweden with Oliver Cromwell, the Protector stated that "already in his youth he favoured King Gustav Adolf and suffered with all the good people that the attitude of England at this time was so perverse, that there was no help for the Swedes from this land. [...] He added to this a lot about his zeal for pure religion and predicted that Charles Gustav could complete the matter Gustav Adolf had started."[12]

Yet another question remains unanswered: if the myth of the Swedish Liberator, the Lion of the North, was strong enough to bear the military and political action at the time of Charles Gustav's accession to the throne. The opinions are different. The research results obtained by Arno Herzig concerning the province of Silesia in the 17th and 18th centuries are worth recalling.[13] They provide us with a

---

[10] Pufendorf, *De rebus*, 4: § 41, trans. W.K.

[11] Pufendorf, *De rebus*, 4: § 42, trans. W.K.

[12] Pufendorf, *De rebus*, 2: § 90, trans. W.K. *Swedish Diplomats at Cromwell's Court. The Missions of Peter Julius Coyet and Christer Bonde*, trans. and ed. Michael Roberts (London: Royal Historical Society,1988), 12, 133, 224.

[13] Arno Herzig, "Die Rezeption Gustav Adolfs in Schlesien," in *Po obu stronach Bałtyku. Wzajemne relacje między Skandynawią a Europą Środkową. On the Opposite Sides of the Baltic*

fine *exemplum*, since this Protestant region was subjected to severe recatholicization both before and after the Thirty Years' War. Herzig shows that the myth of the possible Swedish rescue of the Protestants from the Habsburgs was unstable in Silesia. When Gustav II Adolf was among the living and pursued active policy in the Empire, the expectations were high. At the early stages of war there were no Swedish troops in the region, which was occupied by the Catholic Habsburg forces. But when the Protestant army marched into Silesia, the initial satisfaction of the population soon turned into disaffection. Common religion did not prevent looting and violence. Nonetheless, the myth survived, even in the times after 1648, when Silesia came again under the rule of the Habsburgs.[14]

A pathetic story of erecting the Peace Church (*Friedenskirche*) in Świdnica (Schweidnitz) as well shows a link to Charles X Gustav. In the Peace of Westphalia the Emperor Ferdinand III Habsburg granted minor concessions to the Lutherans living in Silesia. Under the pressure from some states, i.a. Sweden, he agreed that Protestants could build three new churches in Głogów (*Glogau*), Jawór (*Jauer*) and Świdnica (*Schweidnitz*). All the old churches, serving the Protestants for more than a century, were confiscated and returned to the Catholics. There were, however, severe restrictions concerning materials to be used in the construction of the three Peace Churches – only unstable ones, like clay, sand, wood and straw were permitted. The buildings had to be completed within one year and the Protestants had to cover all their costs.[15]

On 5th May 1654 burghers Christian Czepko and Matthäus Scholtz from Świdnica began their arduous journey from their home town to Stockholm. We know a lot about their travel thanks to the Czepko's

Sea. Relations between Scandinavian and Central European Countries, vol. 1, ed. Jan Harasimowicz et al. (Wrocław: Wydawnictwo "Via Nova," 2006), 63–68.

[14]   Piotr Oszczanowski, "'Szwedzka sień' we Wrocławiu, czyli 'dyskretna' apoteoza Gustawa II Adolfa," in *Po obu stronach Bałtyku*, vol. 1, 85.

[15]   Józef Pater, "Kościoły pokoju i łaski przejawem tolerancji religijnej na Śląsku," in *Religia i polityka. Kwestie wyznaniowe i konflikty polityczne w Europie w XVIII wieku*, ed. Lucyna Harc and Gabriela Wąs (Wrocław: Wydawnictwo Uniwersytetu Wrocławskiego, 2009), 151–154.

journal, in which he described all the interesting events.[16] The Lutheran community burdened both men with an important task: to collect the funds needed for the erection of the Peace Church. They hoped that the King of Sweden would assist them in such a noble undertaking. Ultimately, they came to Stockholm in August 1654, admired the Royal Wedding of Charles X Gustav in November, and were "obliged to keep patience." They had to wait up to December for good news. Finally, the King granted a modest subsidy and ordered the governors in Swedish Pomerania and Principality of Bremen "to organize a collection" as well as in the local churches.[17] As is usually the case, the income was not as successful as had been expected. Both travellers did not bring a desired amount of money home, still the Peace Church of Świdnica was erected in the prescribed time and the first service was celebrated on 24th June 1657.[18]

But despite all the neglect, the province of Silesia was not forgotten in Stockholm. During negotiations with France in 1656 Swedish diplomats pointed to this very region, stating that: "It is true that we do not have such important and obvious reasons to complain about the emperor (as the French do), but it is not to be tolerated that so many decisions of the (Westphalia) Peace Treaty were not fulfilled, and, in particular, that the Protestants in Silesia endure such a heavy persecution."[19]

The myth was revived once more in the time of the Great Northern War (1700–1721) by the actions of Charles XII, grandson of

---

[16] Christian Czepko, *Schwedische Reise, Swedish Journey*, intr. Joanna Lamparska, English trans. Anna Bielawska (Świdnica: Parafia Ewangelicko-Augsburska pw. św. Trójcy, 2008); Jörg Deventer, "Protestant Self-Assertion in Silesia after the Peace of Westphalia: The Journey of Christian Czepko from Świdnica to Stockholm (1654/1655)," in *Po obu stronach Bałtyku*, vol. I, 115–120.

[17] Czepko, *Schwedische Reise*, 63.

[18] The monumental Peace Church in Świdnica still exists and in 2001 joined the UNESCO world heritage list. But it is not a museum – despite all the changes and forced resettlement of the German population after 1945, the Lutheran community still owns the buildings and the worship is celebrated.

[19] Pufendorf, *De rebus*, 3: § 60, trans. W.K.

Charles X Gustav.[20] King of Sweden crushed Polish-Lithuanian-Saxon forces and in 1706 proceeded with his army to Saxony to beat his opponent, Augustus II the Strong, King of Poland and Elector of Saxony. The province of Silesia was only a transit area for the Swedish troops. However, Charles XII, well acquainted with the modern history, saw himself as a defender of the Protestants' case and heir to Gustavus Adolphus. In accordance with the Westphalia Treaty, he, as the King of Sweden, was permitted to intervene in the religious matters in Silesia. In fear of war, the Emperor Josef I agreed to serious concessions and on 1st September 1707 the convention was signed in the castle of Altranstädt. Silesian Protestants regained hundred and twenty old churches and were permitted to build six new – so-called Churches of Grace (*Gnadenkirche*).[21]

Contemporary German and Swedish publications raised no doubts – Charles XII was presented both in texts and in pictures as the Lion of the North, the Defender of Protestants, worthy successor of Gustav Adolf and Martin Luther.[22]

More than half a century ago Sven Göransson formulated an opinion that the confessional policy in Europe was in retreat in the years 1654–1660.[23] This view is still defendable, yet some reservations must be made pertaining to the reign of Charles Gustav. It seems that the myth of the Lion of the North was still valued as an important asset in the Swedish policy. However, the war in Poland-Lithuania or in Den-

---

[20] Robert I. Frost, *The Northern Wars. War, State and Society in Northeastern Europe, 1558–1721* (Harlow: Longman, 2000), 263–271.

[21] One of them, the Church of Grace in Jelenia Góra (Hirschberg), is a replica of the magnificent *Katarina kyrka* in Stockholm, built in 1695. Katarina, who was venerated in such a manner, was Princess Catharine of Sweden – Katarina Karlsdotter Vasa, mother of Charles X Gustav. The Church of Grace in Jelenia Góra, the greatest of all the six Churches, was completed in the years 1709–1718. Andrea Langer, "Die Hirschberger Gnadenkirche 'Zum Kreuze Christi' im künstlerischen Spannungsfeld von Noreuropäisch geprägtem Protoklassizismus und römisch geprägtem Barock," in *Po obu stronach Bałtyku*, vol. 1, 203–215.

[22] Otfried Czaika, "Carolus Redivivus oder der wiederaufwachende nordische Löwe – das Bild Karl XII. als Retter des Protestantismus in der proschwedischen Publizistik," in *Religia i polityka*, 57–83.

[23] Sven Göransson, *Den europeiska konfessionspolitikens upplösning, 1654–1660, Religion och utrikespolitik under Karl X Gustav* (Uppsala–Wiesbaden: Uppsala Universitets Årsskrift, 1956).

mark did not stand a chance of using it. On the contrary, the King of Sweden tried hard to avoid the impression that the invasion of the Commonwealth had something in common with religious matters. Nonetheless, the Polish side, and the royal court in particular, made efforts, not without success, to change the dynastic conflict into the religious war. The context was somewhat different when it comes to the Swedish policy against the Holy Empire, where Charles Gustav had been considering the intervention, which may be exemplified by hints given in *De rebus*.

The commander

On 5th May 1656 French chief minister, Cardinal Mazarin, wrote a lengthy letter to victorious Charles Gustav on the order of Louis XIV. The tone was of course amicable, but there was also a clear critical note hidden in baroque phrases. The King of France was surprised at the actions of the King of Sweden on the battlefield. Let us recall these words:

> He [Mazarin] cannot hide two sentiments which deeply permeated the Frenchmen towards him [i.e. Charles Gustav]. The first one is admiration for the evidence of his extraordinary courage, but the second is the concern about the constant dangers in which he permanently exposes his head. [Mazarin] knows well enough how important the presence of the monarch is for the army, which fights before his very eyes and follows an example of his bravery. However, it is also obvious that the fate of the whole kingdom, or sometimes of many [kingdoms], is dependent on the life of one, brave and wise king. Therefore, oftentimes it must be preserved and everything else must be put at risk, and it is just to keep this [life] safe, outside the blows of violent actions. Good stars are not deprived of their salutary effect just because they are a bit more distant. Then, if the welfare of so many people is dependent upon the King's life, so he [Mazarin] does not hesitate to claim that if [the king] does not spare himself more, he will risk the good of many, which belongs more to them than to him. He should tame his lust for fame, which is his natural disposition, for the love of his subjects, for his Royal House, and for his allies. In such a manner he will achieve the victory over himself, which certainly will cost him more effort than the triumph over the foe. But this [victory] has to be valued higher than the

former, although it comes without the din. [Mazarin] writes it at his King's [Louis XIV] special command.[24]

It was a sharp rebuke, yet was it just? Louis XIV, despite all the martial paintings and sculptures, was not the first line fighter as he rather encouraged his marshals to take command in the battles and only later savoured their victories. Most probably he recognized acts of Charles Gustav's personal bravery as his infantile lust for fame. In his eyes the potential benefits for the army's morale could not outweigh the risks. The experience of the King of Sweden was entirely different. Under orders from the Swedish Field Marshall Lennart Torstenson, he participated in several battles of the Thirty Years' War; notably in Lepizig in 1642, where he commanded a deciding attack, and at the very bloody encounter in Jankov in 1645.[25] However, these brave actions were rather a manifestation of the Swedish style of command than wanton bravado. When facing that 17th-century battle, Bo Eriksson in his book *Lützen 1632* described convincingly different problems of a commanding general.[26] A lack of communication, disorientation were all-too-common and could lead to the wrong assessment of the situation. Yet a strong leader could turn the tide of the encounter with one resolute decision. The King as commander-in-chief had as well this great advantage, specifically that his orders were undisputed, and consequently he could shorten the time of response to the emerging threat.

It is characteristic that the first and at the same time victorious stage of the war in Poland in 1655 does not provide us with information about the direct involvement of Charles Gustav in the actions on the battlefields, where the King could be endangered and did some real fighting himself. We see him as a supervisor and planner. The situation changed when the problems emerged. In the winter and

---

[24] Pufendorf, *De rebus*, 3: § 60, trans. W.K.

[25] Stellan Dahlgren, "Karl X Gustav," in *Svenskt Biografiskt Lexikon*, vol. 20, ed. Erik Grill (Stockholm 1973–1975), 641–643; Peter Englund, *Ofredsår. Om den svenska stormaktstiden och en man i dess mitt* (Stockholm: Atlantis, 2001), 260–263, 383–390; Jerzy Maroń, *Wokół teorii rewolucji militarnej. Wybrane problemy* (Wrocław: Wydawnictwo Uniwersytetu Wrocławskiego, 2011), 78–79, 90–91.

[26] Bo Eriksson, *Lützen 1632. Ett ödesdigert beslut* (Stockholm: Norstedts, 2006), 277–281.

early spring of 1656 Charles Gustav had Stefan Czarniecki, master of raids and guerrilla warfare, as his main opponent. "Throughout the whole war Czarniecki was the most annoying enemy for the Swedes, unexpectedly attacking here and there with light troops, stirring up the folk everywhere, supplying his forces with the nobles, who joined him."[27] During the retreat from the land of Przemyśl, skirmishes occurred frequently, some of which developed into serious clashes, like the one close to the town of Jarosław:[28]

> To stand secure in this town, the King decided to fortify the suburbs in order to accommodate the whole army. [Swedes] immediately started to work. Three hundred soldiers were designated to accomplish this task, since half a mile from the town there was a narrow passage where it was necessary to build an earthwork as a protection against a sudden attack of the enemy. Czarniecki suddenly raided them from the nearby forest, and after a clash, which lasted an hour, destroyed Colonel Braun, who came out to meet him with three hundred horses, killing forty of the cavalry and many workers. Meanwhile, a large part of them [workers] fled across the bridge over the San river near Jarosław. If not for the vigilance and bravery of the King, who first mounted his horse and moved quickly at the head of infantry, Czarniecki would have burst over the bridge into the camp almost together with Braun and would have undoubtedly caused great confusion. But when the bullets fired from the muskets began to whistle near the ears of the Poles, Czarniecki turned his troops quickly and fled in a disturbed order through the narrow passages into the forest losing a few companies. The King hurriedly gathered a few regiments of cavalry, except for the Polish regiment, ordered Wittenberg to follow him, and commenced to chase Czarniecki. Many of those escaping, who stayed behind, were killed. The pursuit lasted till late evening, more than one and a half mile,[29] accordingly, the King could not return to the camp for the night.[30]

The Swedish army continued its march, which was becoming more and more difficult owing to snowmelt and muddy, narrow roads. Two weeks after that encounter near Jarosław, a new dangerous situation unfolded near the town of Nisko, well protected by water obstacles:

> But in the early evening, when a greater number of the Swedish cavalrymen left the camp to collect fodder, while other regiments dismounted, Czarniecki, cunning

---

[27] Pufendorf, *De rebus*, 3: § 5.

[28] The best description of this campaign is to be found in Andrzej Borcz, *Przemyśl 1656–1657* (Warszawa: Dom Wydawniczy "Bellona," 2006).

[29] The old Swedish mile (from 1649) was approximately 10,689 metres, so the road of the pursuit could amount to c. 15 kilometres

[30] Pufendorf, *De rebus*, 3: § 8, trans. W.K.

and fast, fell out from the nearby forest with several thousand, mainly nobles and drove fifty of the cavalry to the camp, those who stood as the outermost and main guards. The King, who as one of the first heard the racket, fired two cannons with his own hands, giving a signal [for the battle to begin], and ordered the drummers to sound the alarm. Then he mounted his horse and led the attack consisting of his guard and other regiments against the enemy. In this way he stopped the momentum of the foe, who could otherwise disturb the whole camp.[31]

But this was not the end of troubles. In the last days of March the whole Swedish army got stuck in the narrow place where the rivers San and Vistula meet. The enemy was everywhere, sure of victory. In a bold action (which will be described in the chapter to follow) the Swedes crossed the San river and crushed the opposing Lithuanian forces. The fire was fierce and "one cannonball flew between the King's legs, not causing any harm, only covering his face and clothing with dust."[32]

Charles Gustav occasionally embarked on dangerous scouting expeditions – similarly to Gustav Adolf.[33] In December 1656 he crossed the Vistula river through the ice floe to conduct the reconnaissance, but due to the melting snow and bridge near Grudziądz (Graudentz) that was destroyed, he could not return to his army and had to wait until the bridge had been repaired.[34]

If Louis XIV had heard of that expedition, which he most probably had, he must have been confused. In the period of one month the King of Sweden rescued his own army three times. Was he conducting reconnaissance in person? The worst news was yet to come. "In Vienna, Wrocław and Gdańsk (*Danzig*) pamphlets were printed with such detailed descriptions of the Swedish defeat and King's of Sweden death that you could infer that the authors were witnesses to these events. Many believed in these lies so long that they freed themselves from them only when two years later they saw the King

---

[31] Pufendorf, *De rebus*, 3: § 9, trans. W.K.
[32] Pufendorf, *De rebus*, 3: § 12, trans. W.K.
[33] Michael Roberts, *Gustavus Adolphus. A History of Sweden 1611–1632*, vol. 2 (Edinburgh: Longmans, Green & Co., 1957), 557.
[34] Pufendorf, *De rebus*, 3: § 39, trans. W.K.

alive in Hamburg."[35] Meanwhile, because of the news, important negotiations had to be discontinued for months, since everyone was waiting for its confirmation. It seems that the Polish side was much better at propaganda warfare than the Swedes.

Sometimes the courageous behaviour of the King was well thought out. After first victories, when many Polish troops joined the Swedish army, Charles Gustav treated them as his own soldiers, or at least pretended that it was so. "The King did not hesitate to appear leisurely in their (Polish) camps in the company of only a few of his guardians and walked there almost without any fear."[36] Of course, the king needed these experienced units – they were especially valuable for reconnaissance – and wanted to win their goodwill. When in 1656 the situation changed to the detriment of the Swedes, the Polish troops were used quite cynically:

> When the King found that he was no longer safe from the enemy attacks, he decided that in order to prevent it, he would send a strong squad ahead of the main forces. He hesitated, however, whether to send his own troops to such a dangerous position, because they could easily be killed while being encircled by the foe. Therefore, he selected Jan Sapieha and his [Polish] 'quarter' soldiers to follow the King's task. If he wanted to escape, he would inflict less damage than if he was to disturb the ranks in the battle. Hence [Sapieha] was ordered to stay ahead about two miles of the rest of the army. Consequently, there would be no big loss if some of his [Polish] subordinates were killed. Because of the uproar, the King would gain some time to set the forces for the battle.[37]

A dangerous situation could occur suddenly. In early May the Swedish army tried to capture enemy outposts near Gdańsk. One of them was the *Gutlander Schantze* near Steblewo, over a dozen kilometres from the town.[38] "The besieged, as if gripped by fear, hung out the white flag on the rampart and stopped shooting. The King believed that they were ready to surrender and rode horseback to the earthwork in the company of Stenbock. Then the besieged fired at

---

[35] Pufendorf, *De rebus*, 3: § 12, trans. W.K.
[36] Pufendorf, *De rebus*, 3: § 32, trans. W.K.
[37] Pufendorf, *De rebus*, 3: § 10, trans. W.K.
[38] Jerzy Stankiewicz, "System fortyfikacyjny Gdańska i okolicy w czasie wojny 1655 1660 r.," *Studia i Materiały do Historii Wojskowości*, vol. 20 (1976), 115–116.

them from two pointed guns, yet missed, so they were only covered with the dust. In response, the King signalled to his men to attack the traitors."[39]

Already in July 1656 a fierce, three-day battle of Warsaw took place and the King's life was endangered once more. The unclear circumstances of this event will be discussed in the next chapter.

There was a certain pattern of the King's behaviour – in difficult situations he preferred to lead the fights – like his great predecessor Gustavus Adolphus. While crossing the frozen Belt straits on 30th January 1658, he accompanied his troops where several squads and his personal sledges fell under the broken ice. Moments later, by Iversnæs, the Swedish and Danish infantry clashed on the ice. "In this battle the Danes began to shoot early at the approaching Swedes, and one great cannonball hit the ground just in front of the King's horse, so that the snow showered his face and Quartermaster-general Dahlbergh's."[40]

However, we can find also some incidents which are incomprehensible in our age. On 7th April 1657 the Swedish army with their allies, Transylvanians and Cossacks, began to cross the Vistula river:

> When the King, accompanied by [Prince] Rákóczy and his suite, reached a small island to examine the location, some Polish troops, from the opposite shore, who wanted to prevent the construction of the bridge, fired from their muskets at the Swedes, who were not slow at their response. So, the King's companions warned him not to ride towards the gunshot. Oblivious to the danger, he moved on. The Colonel Korycki, Pole who remained loyal to the King to the very end, ran to the riverbank and summoned his countrymen; he pointed towards the King of Sweden to prevent from hurting him. The Poles, to show politeness of their nation, especially officers and nobles, dismounted at once and bareheaded bowed several times honouring the King in such a way. Soon after they mounted their horses again, but covered their heads only when they went out of King's sight. To respond with the same courtesy, the King prohibited to shoot at them.[41]

Without a doubt Charles Gustav was a very good tactician, but the question remains if he was a good strategist too. In this regard

---

[39] Pufendorf, *De rebus*, 3: § 17, trans. W.K.
[40] Pufendorf, *De rebus*, 5: § 5, trans. W.K. See also Lars Ericson Wolke, *1658 Tåget över Bält* (Lund: Historiska Media, 2008), 121–123.
[41] Pufendorf, *De rebus*, 4: § 14, trans. W.K.

Pufendorf went quite far in criticizing King's decisions. He writes directly that the attempt to control whole Poland was doomed from the very beginning: "The cautious [people] thought, however, that the King gave himself to first victories, much more than it was appropriate. [...] If the forces were to extend over a wide area, they would weaken as watercourse that loses its power in a broad riverbed." The King should pursue a more modest prey and to focus primarily on the coastal provinces – like the Royal (Polish) Prussia. And who is to be blamed for the greed and failure? "Such moderate and cautious advice was, as usual, rejected with contempt and arrogance by the people of the war-craft and others."[42]

Of course there is such a possibility that Pufendorf interpreted the archival sources in King's favour. There are no simple answers, and actually each case must be examined separately. Sometimes, however, we can reveal a tendency to justify King's actions – not infrequently in Pufendorf's tale the Swedish aristocrats are scapegoats, guilty of incitement to some erroneous resolves. The best example of such misrepresentation of sources is the Pufendorf's account of the alleged deliberations in Kiel in 1658, where the major decisions were taken by the Swedish council of war how to attack Denmark. Pufendorf stresses that Charles Gustav "calculated that the whole fleet was to head for Copenhagen, where [the ships] were to enter the port and the infantry was to land in the middle of the town. The said plan seemed too bold, nonetheless, it could have succeeded if only fearless spirit had been fostered and a blow dealt, granted that the Danes would not have eliminated the initial confusion and in the town [of Copenhagen] nothing would have been ready for defence. But the plan was rejected unanimously by all the generals under the pretext that it could not have succeeded and if [the Swedes] had incurred some defeat in the first attack, the whole expedition would have come to a standstill. Therefore, it was decided to land in Korsør."[43] So far so good. However, in 1927 Torsten Holm published an exact protocol of

---

[42] Pufendorf, *De rebus*, 3: § 1, trans. W.K.
[43] Pufendorf, *De rebus*, 5: § 95, trans. W.K.

the meeting, dated at 24th June 1658 – most probably the council was not held in Kiel. It contains statements of participants and is a rare example of an accurate recording of a debate at the time.[44] It clearly shows that all the members of the council agreed on Korsør, and, furthermore, the landing in Copenhagen was not addressed at all.

The ultimate test of King's courage was his final hours on earth. A description of the circumstances of the monarch's death was published customarily at the time, and served as an additional confirmation both of magnificence of the ruler and his Christian piety.[45]

> [Charles Gustav] ordered a doctor to warn him several hours before he was to die. After the doctor's reminder, he wished to be transferred from the bed to the chair by the table and wanted his last will to be read in the presence of some members of the Council of the Realm. Then he asked whether there was anyone who thought that the document was improper. When nobody answered, he signed it with his own hand. Subsequently, he signed other letters and documents, and finally, he rewarded his distinguished ministers. Having completed all the arrangements, as if weary of a struggle, he called for silence, and when those gathered asked him to go back to bed, [the King] stated that once he returned there, he would die, but nevertheless he had to face it. His fearless spirit that manifested itself throughout his life, did not leave him until the end. He was moved to bed and after entrusting his soul to the Creator and Saviour, without any signs of pain, he sighed slightly and departed this life in the arms of the Marshal, Count Gabriel Oxenstierna and Count Niklas Brahe, about two hours after midnight.[46]

However, the King's last will was changed almost immediately by the members of the Council of the Realm. Pufendorf diligently reports this fact, he makes another accusation of the aristocratic regents governing Sweden after Charles X Gustav's premature departure.

---

[44] Torsten Holm, *Översikt över Sveriges krig under 1600-talets senare hälvt* (Stockholm: Militärlitteraturföreningens Förlag, 1927), 205–206. See also Stade, *Erik Dahlbergh och Carl X Gustafs krigshistoria. Carl Gustaf Studier*, vol. 3 (Kristianstad: Militärhistoriska Förlaget, 1967), 328. Stade calls the council in Kiel "apocryphal."

[45] Bo Bennich-Björkman, *Författaren i ämbetet. Studier i funktion och organisation av författarämbeten vid svenska hovet och kansliet 1550–1850* (Uppsala: Studia litterarum Upsaliensia, 1970), 297.

[46] Pufendorf, *De rebus*, 7: § 2, trans. W.K.

The face of war

On 1st April 1657 a small detachment of the Swedish horse under the command of Quartermaster Lieutenant Erik Dahlbergh was sent to arrange accommodation for the army in the village Kobylany near the Krzyżtopór castle. This was an important day for the Swedes, since their long expected ally, the Transylvanian prince George II Rákóczy, had already arrived with his troops. Yet Pufendorf suddenly changes the said theme:

> [Dahlbergh] found a Pole lying on his back, his heart was pierced by two bullets, eyes closed, bloody foam flowed from his mouth. The soldiers decided that it would be humane to reduce the suffering of the wounded, since there was no hope for his survival. One of them jumped off the horse, pointed the handgun at his forehead and fired, the brain leaked out. Then the injured put his right hand on the wound, slipped his fingers into the blood and brain. At that time other soldiers shot twice, hitting the wounded between eyes, breaking off the upper part of the skull. Despite this, the Pole was still moving his fingers in the wound. The Swede stabbed him then in the heart with his rapier three or four times. With each thrust the Pole pulled up his legs and put his hands on his chest. He was stabbed many times from the stomach to the neck. Numerous bullets pierced his head and heart, the blood flowed from the broken skull, but he still moved his legs and arms, and began to moan quietly, as if he wanted to say something. Everyone present was surprised that he was still alive, when his heart and forehead were punctured so many times. They observed this occurrence for half an hour and finally left him, not dead yet.[47]

This is a clear interpolation in the narrative, which does not fit well to the previous description of major events. Suddenly, we are moved to a small village to meet a wounded Pole and a Swedish quartermaster's unit. It is as well striking that we do not notice soldiers' hatred towards the defeated enemy. They do not humiliate him. In fact, they try to help. Latin words used to describe their motivation are *humanitatis officium*, which can be translated into *humanitarian service*. The killing and dying seems to be a very laborious and slow process, contrary to what the news, films and computer games of our age present.

---

[47]   Pufendorf, *De rebus*, 4: § 11, trans. W.K. The scene is, however, based on the shorter description by Erik Dahlbergh. Arne Stade, *Erik Dahlbergh*, 194.

After the Thirty Years' War such horrors were a frequent theme in the literature and art of the seventeenth century.[48] We will find similar scenes depicted in the etchings of Jacques Callot or Karel Dujardin. Or, we can also consider it to be a description of curiosity. Historians as well commented this event. Ludwik Kubala, who was likewise struck by this scene, offered yet another explanation: "this tormented man represented Poland, which the enemy was not capable of defeating."[49] Arne Stade, after the examination of the Dahlbergh's manuscript, noted that the episode with the wounded Pole was added later, thus it may constitute the Dahlbergh's invention.[50] Peter Englund remarked that such behaviour towards the wounded was normal at the time, as there were no adequate medical services available.[51]

However, there is still disagreement concerning the main subject of the Pufendorf's work. The author knows about it, he starts his description with the following words: "forte non indignum memoratu est...," also: "perhaps it is not unworthy to mention." He had to depict deeds of Charles Gustav, but what does this episode have to do with the King's deeds?

But maybe it does. Is that torment and agony not caused directly by the King's actions? Despite all the descriptions of King's courage and magnanimity, we are confronted as well with the brutal reality of war in *De rebus*. In the same chapter we find a description of festivities related to the arrival of the Prince Rákóczy's army. Nonetheless, "this joy was disturbed considerably by the death of Duke Adolf of Nassau, who, was hit on the head with bullet fired by one of his men as he stood in front of his regiment of horse. No one knew whether it was an accident or a deliberate action." Yet another reminder of the real situation around.

---

[48] Klaus Hoppe, "Die Greuel des Krieges," in *30järiger Krieg, Münster und der Westfälische Frieden*, vol. 1 (Münster: Stadtmuseum Münster, 1998), 145–166.

[49] Ludwik Kubala, *Wojna brandenburska i najazd Rakoczego w roku 1656 i 1657* (Lwów–Warszawa: Biblioteka Historyczna Altenberga, 1917), 1.

[50] Stade, *Erik Dahlbergh*, 194.

[51] Peter Englund, *Den oövervinnerlige. Om de svenska stormaktstiden och en man i dess mitt* (Stockholm: Atlantis, 2000), 461.

It should be stressed that similar examples of atrocities of war are not very common in the Pufendorf's work, but still we can perceive the Author's plan: to show the suffering and cruelty of the bloody conflict, not only the exhilaration of victories. By way of illustration, a few specific pictures may be presented.

During the suppression of the revolt in Lithuania in 1656 the Swedes did not treat the foe gently – quite probably because the enemy forces were composed of mainly peasants, despised by professional soldiers. Describing the clash in the village of Gruździe, Pufendorf mentions:

> Initially, the rebels kept the position and tried to fight. However, our [Swedes] drove them soon to the village and forced to flee. Since they had to break through our troops, most were pierced by the bullets while escaping or when they were in the swamps. Only a few managed to escape. Most of the infantry was wiped out in the village. When they saw our attacking forces, they dropped their weapons and squeezed like a flock of sheep exposing their bodies. Of two thousand peasants who were caught there, five hundred were sent to the town of Riga where they had to work on the shafts. A few were released so that they could tell others about the fruit of rebellion. All the others lost their lives.[52]

The prisoners of war of low origin were not especially valuable and were rather something to get rid of. After heavy fighting in Finland, "Lewenhaupt arranged the matters so that the Russians could not penetrate the area any deeper, consequently, the troops, circulating everywhere, took a great number of prisoners. Since they were of no use and the tsar did not want any ransom or exchange, they were killed."[53] Every side of this conflict acted with increasing cruelty. At the end of 1655 the rebels in Poland attacked the town of Wieluń, inhabited mainly by the Protestants:

"At night when the Swedes were asleep [the rebels] entered the town and quietly killed the guards at the gate. They opened it and let their troops in. There were so many Swedes in the town that they would be enough to repel the Poles if only they could take up arms and gather in one place. But the Poles rapidly occupied the streets and

---

52 Pufendorf, *De rebus*, 3: § 46, trans. W.K,
53 Pufendorf, *De rebus*, 3: § 49, trans. W.K.

raising a terrible cry killed everyone they met outside so that everybody sought refuge. When the daytime came, the Poles dismounted, broke into the homes and murdered all the German-speaking inhabitants, making no difference between soldiers, craftsmen, or travellers."[54] Here follows a precise description of different horrors and cruelties seen in the captured town. Such a "linguistic" way to distinguish the friend from the foe had a long "tradition" in Poland. In 1312, when the troops of Prince Władysław Łokietek entered rebellious Kraków, those burghers who could not pronounce *soczewica* (Eng. *lentil*), *koło* (Eng. *wheel*), *miele* (Eng. *grind*), *młyn* (Eng. *mill*) lost their lives.[55]

Wojciech Łygaś has recently studied a folk legend on the castle of Gołańcz in the province of Greater Poland (Wielkopolska). It says that a beautiful daughter of a Polish castellan saved her countrymen in the time of the Swedish invasion, later, however, she committed suicide.[56] As usual, there is a grain of truth in the legend. Polish sources confirm that the castle was beset by the Swedes in the spring of 1656. All the nearby houses were burned and destroyed, all Poles who sought refuge in the castle were killed, the wife of the rebellious voivode Grudziński was wounded, her two sons hacked to death. Pufendorf describes this in such a way:

> It was reported that in the nearby castle of Gołańcz a castellan and a handful of nobles and two hundred of peasants were planning something hostile. Therefore, it was decided that a troop of horse and dragoons were to be sent to call them to order. At the request to surrender, [the Poles] fired at the Swedes and injured some. Four cannons were brought immediately, which smashed the gates of the castle.

---

[54] Pufendorf, *De rebus*, 3: § 14, trans. W. K. Pufendorf's story is an abridged translation of the German propaganda pamphlet published shortly after the events. However, it agrees well with the subsequent research, see: Wiesław Sauter, *Krzysztof Żegocki, pierwszy partyzant Rzeczypospolitej 1618–1673* (Poznań: Wydawnictwo Poznańskie, 1981), 82–85. The pamphlet can be found at the site of *Digital Library of Polish and Poland-Related News Pamphlets from the 16th to the 18th Centuries*: http://cbdu.id.uw.edu.pl/6060/1/Z606.djvu [4 June 2014].

[55] The meaning is: *lentil, wheel, grind, mill*, respectively. Such words were used, for they are difficult to pronounce for people unfamiliar with the Polish language. Jerzy Wyrozumski, *Dzieje Krakowa*, vol. 1: *Kraków do schyłku wieków średnich* (Kraków: Wydawnictwo Literackie, 1992), 202.

[56] Wojciech Łygaś, *Szwedzkie opowieści. Z dziejów polsko-szwedzkich XIV–XVIII w.* (Gdańsk: Finna, 2005), 231–240.

The Swedes moved at once, not giving time to those beleaguered to destroy the bridge. They overthrew the stockade, lowered the drawbridge, broke into the castle and killed everyone carrying the weapon they met. Major General Bülow took care that the women were not raped. They were taken to the camp, where prince [Adolf Johan] released them safely and without any ransom.[57]

In 2009 and 2010 a group of archaeologists under the direction of Artur Różański and Tomasz Olszacki conducted excavations in the Gołańcz castle.[58] They found a shallow collective grave filled with skeletons, where skulls of some victims were smashed with stones. A part of the burial ground has not been excavated yet. And there are many such places in Poland, Denmark, Finland, or Lithuania.

Blaming the king

The question arises, in fact, whether Pufendorf could and wanted to criticize the King. If we answer affirmatively, we should as well ask: how far he could go and what methods he used. The above-mentioned descriptions of atrocities may only reflect the contemporary ways of presenting the war. They cannot be directly perceived as reproach directed at Charles Gustav. As a matter of fact, Pufendorf, the *Historiographer of the Kingdom*, was expected to write a praise of the King, not a reprimand, of which he was, undeniably, aware. A careful reading of his work reveals, however, a clever tactic he deployed when he was to describe difficult issues, in which the king's case was not unambiguous.

Thus, Pufendorf quotes abundantly statements of the opponents of Charles Gustav and Sweden. Obviously, he also presents Swedish counterarguments, but quite often they are simply weaker. In such a way the Author could protect himself and describe inconvenient facts and opinions. In the *First book* of *De rebus*, § 50, there is an ac-

---

[57] Pufendorf, *De rebus*, 3: § 16, trans. W.K.
[58] The article of Wojciech Pastuszka is available from: http://archeowiesci.pl/2010/09/21/o zamku-w-golanczy-i-masowej-mogile-z-czasow-potopu-raz-jeszcze/ [4 June 2014].

curate account of the proceedings of the Swedish War Council, which took place from 8th to 12th December 1654 (Old Style). The anti-war arguments were well chosen and presented first. The supporters of peace pointed out that in the time of the Thirty Years' War Sweden had many friends and foes which underestimated the Swedish power, there was a great confusion in the Grand Duchy of Muscovy, and the war in Germany was fought by the Swedish troops composed mainly of the Germans. Nonetheless, in 1654 the situation was completely different. Also, they were not to expose Sweden to obvious danger while trying to prevent a potential threat.[59] Characteristic are as well the arguments for the war described in the § 51, ergo let us quote just one passage: "even if the word 'peace' is so sweet, it would cost too much, if the price was respect, security and growth of the kingdom. However, strengthening the troops and adding mercenaries from abroad to the permanent regiments just to keep them in idleness would mean war with ourselves and would bring about a devastating effect. And there is nothing more harmful than the expenses that are incurred on too numerous and unnecessary soldiers, who are idle, for they should not be fed for free. Since lasting peace brings effeminacy to the soldiers, they become unable to bear the hardships of war and the martial spirit of the nation becomes weaker, long wars, in contrast, nurtures it." Stronger and more convincingly sounds the opinion of the Swedish Parliament (*Riksdag*) expressed by Pufendorf at the beginning of the *Second book*:

> After considering the matters, the members of Riksdag expressed their view: the value of the arms of the Russians and Poles should not be underestimated. First of all, however, we should consider what necessity compels us to start war immediately, and whether these are sufficient reasons for our decision. The treaties stipulated that if any offence was initiated, we should approach a friendly way first. The representatives of the states do not hide their opinion and would like to postpone the war and keep the king at home to effectively administer the affairs of the state of the kingdom so far neglected.[60]

---

[59] Arne Stade, while analyzing the protocols indicated that the deliberations were stormy and the opposition to the war plans quite strong. Arne Stade, "Geneza decyzji Karola X Gustawa o wojnie z Polską w 1655 r.," *Studia i Materiały do Historii Wojskowości*, vol. XIX, part 2 (1973): 23.

[60] Pufendorf, *De rebus*, 2: § 7, trans. W.K.

The imbalance of the presented arguments appears most clearly in the description of the meeting of Charles Gustav with Kazimierz Przy-jemski, the messenger of the King John Casimir.[61] It took place on 16th August 1655 when the Swedish army was already in Poland and enjoyed its first victories. Przyjemski was a deliberate choice – the said Polish courtier served once in the Swedish army under the King Gustavus Adolphus, as did his brother Sigismund Przyjemski. The speech that he delivered to the Swedish king was an excellent display of oratorical skills. At the beginning, he talked about the surprise of the Polish King John Casimir: why the truce was broken by the Swedes and why they came with an army to such a peaceful country. The provisions of the truce were not violated by the Polish side, which abstained from the participation in the Thirty Years' War in order not to offend the Swedes. Many Poles, as Przyjemski did himself, fought at the Swedish side or supported the King of France, the main ally of Charles Gustav. Did the Swedes feel offended by the wrong titles and inadequate seals used by the Polish Crown Chancery? Even if, "it was not the reason for going to war"! Or else, they were attracted by the lust of plunder? If this was the case, they would soon be disap-pointed, since the Kingdom of Poland was devastated by long wars with the Cossacks and Muscovy. All property of the Poles was based on an annual income from the soil and cattle, and these had been exhausted by their own armies and the armies of their enemy: "the land lie fallow, no one pays taxes and there is hunger everywhere." And further: "What a glory is to invade those who are fighting for their lives against the most terrible enemy?" Charles Gustav should not believe that he could keep hold of Poland with gentle rule – he would need swords and crosses in the land seized with weapon. He should also immediately return to the negotiations.

The reply of the Swedes, presented by the diplomat Matthias Biörenklou, was brief and terse: John Casimir was warned, and as

---

[61] Pufendorf, *De rebus*, 2: § 21.

the testimonies of the Polish wrongdoing were already shown to the world, it was unnecessary to discuss the matter any further.[62]

Undeniably, Pufendorf tried to explain some unworthy actions of Charles Gustav, to wit the incident with the Transylvanian Prince Rákóczy, who was abandoned by the Swedes and suffered a terrible defeat. His army, more than eleven thousand soldiers, was completely crushed by the Tatars in the summer of 1657. Just a few months before the Prince crossed the Carpathians lured by the promises of Charles Gustav.[63] However, the King of Sweden decided soon that it would be better to attack Denmark than to be stuck in Poland. Chapter 22 of the Book IV of *De rebus* is entitled "The King denies blame for the Rákóczy's defeat," where Pufendorf gathers numerous arguments, yet not convincing when compared with the accusations levelled by the Prince: "He ruled his country in peace. The Poles incited him against the Swedes promising great benefits. The Emperor, Russians and Tatars threatened him. However, for the glory of God and because of the love for the King [of Sweden], he neglected it all, made an alliance with the King and marched in the middle of the winter through the toughest roads to complete the alliance. Now, when threatened by the whole power of Poles and the incoming Austrian aid, he was left alone. Only then did he see that the predictions of his wife and others in Transylvania were true: that he would be deceived by the Swedes. The Hungarian chancellor, sent to him by the Emperor, thought likewise. Only then did he notice that the Swedes thought only about their own benefits and he was abandoned in the middle of the sea without any boat and oars."[64]

Charles Gustav also faced severe criticism as a consequence of his fiscal policy during the war. In 1655 he established a special sea duty near Gdańsk, in hope of achieving similar gains to Gustav Adolf during the Prussian war.[65] But history was not to repeat itself. "This tax

---

[62] Pufendorf, *De rebus*, 2: § 22.
[63] The most recent study on the topic is the book by Marcin Markowicz, *Najazd Rakoczego na Polskę* (Zabrze: Inforteditions, 2011).
[64] Pufendorf, *De rebus*, 4: § 29, trans. by W.K.
[65] Roberts, *Gustavus Adolphus*, vol. 2, 80.

brought a lot of dislike for the king and only a small profit, because burghers of Gdańsk abolished their customs duty. By contrast, when sailing into the Strait of Öresund, the Dutch heard about this tax, avoided Gdańsk and sent their vessels to other places."[66] Pufendorf complains even more bitterly about the proceedings of the Swedish tax collectors in Norway: "they demanded the payment of duties with great ferocity, and especially of cod, on which the trade in these towns relied, the collectors searched desperately for the smallest things. It was believed that if at first they could be content with modest fee, they would easily attract the trade from other places of Norway."[67] But the needs of the fiscal-military state were insatiable. In the opinion of the Danes expressed in 1655: "in Sweden all the states were greatly oppressed by extraordinary taxes and duties, and the greater part of the nobility was angry, for they lost goods they once received from the Crown."[68]

The interferences

We have to remember that Pufendorf had to submit his text to the formal acceptance, which meant a possibility of interventions and alterations, which, in turn, could change the tone of the work. Therefore, when assessing *De rebus*, we should as well take notice of the said problem. How far did the interventions reach? What drew attention of the censors? Was any pressure exerted, apart from the official actions?

A special committee was established to review the work.[69] It consisted of Johan Bergenhielm, Counsellor of the Court, professor of history at the Uppsala University and a friend of Pufendorf, and Thomas Polus, Counsellor and Secretary of the Swedish Royal Chan-

---

[66] Pufendorf, *De rebus*, 2: § 18, trans. by W.K.
[67] Pufendorf, *De rebus*, 5: § 107, trans. by W.K.
[68] Pufendorf, *De rebus*, 2: § 82, trans. by W.K.
[69] Stade, *Erik Dahlbergh*, 15, 353.

cery. Bergenhielm's epigrams can be found in some illustrations of *De rebus*, hence we can infer that he was sympathetic to the author and his work. Most likely the interventions from this side were not substantial.

However, one fragment of *De rebus* was deleted on demand of the King Charles XI.[70] It was a statement of Charles Gustav made on the council of war that he always wanted to consult his decisions with the Council of the Realm (*Riksrådet*). Pufendorf states: "It is an excellent example of modesty, although [the King] himself had excellent ideas, he willingly listened, allowed the opinion of others and also wanted that the freedom of expression of the members of the Council of the Realm remained intact." Charles XI introduced absolute government in Sweden at the time when *De rebus* was written, i.e. in the early eighties of the seventeenth century. He did not wish to make even the minor concession in his recently assumed authority, even if it meant censoring of the work devoted to the deeds of his father. Notwithstanding, the text was not read carefully. Very similar passage in the First Book, chapter 50, describing a meeting of the Council of the Realm on the war matters of the Kingdom of Sweden, was not removed: "When the case had to be considered [Charles Gustav] decided that it would be better if he did not appear in person at the Council – to leave more freedom of discussion, and that its members did not complain that the duty of obedience was imposed upon them when they realized what the King desired." Charles Gustav's efforts to achieve a consensus interact here with Pufendorf's view on the essence of state – the ruler may be a representative of the society provided that he has obtained the appropriate consent. Only then can the monarch decide on the reasons of state.[71]

---

[70] The deleted text was printed by Carl Gustaf Warmholtz in *Bibliotheca Historica Sveo-Gothica; eller förteckning uppå så väl trykte som handskifne Böcker, Tractater och Skrifter, hvilka handla om Svenska Historien, eller därutinnan kunna gifva Ljus; Med Critiska och historiska Anmärkningar*, part 9 (Uppsala 1803), 123.

[71] Henryk Olszewski, "Myśli o państwie Samuela Pufendorfa," in *Władza i społeczeństwo. Prace ofiarowane Antoniemu Mączakowi w sześćdziesiątą rocznicę urodzin*, ed. Marcin Kamler et al. (Warszawa: Państwowe Wydawnictwo Naukowe, 1989), 123.

In addition to these official actions of censorship, Pufendorf had to endure attacks of the Swedish generals and officials, which he did not praise enough or even dared to criticize. At the end of his life he was very disappointed about Sweden and felt deeply hurt by his enemies. He believed that an influential group was trying to delay the printing of *De rebus*. He was of the opinion that the protection of Charles XI he was offered was not sufficient, therefore he had to leave the country.[72] But the truth is that in *De rebus* the aristocrats became the scapegoats and were held responsible for nearly all mistakes and failures committed under the reign of Charles Gustav.

There is one more factor worth further investigation. In 1688 Pufendorf, following the invitation of Friedrich Wilhelm, Elector of Brandenburg, moved to the Prussian court and was appointed state historiographer and privy councillor. The question arises whether and to what extent this new affiliation could affect his work on *De rebus*?

Conclusion

While describing the negotiations in London in 1656, Pufendorf noted that it was John Milton, the poet, who translated on the English side.[73] The same Milton who believed that military heroes are in fact in close connection with Satan himself, who loves the glory of war and is fighting with the God as his major foe.[74] Nothing can be worse than such a military pride of cruel actions. Would Pufendorf agree with this opinion?

Formally, *De rebus* is Charles Gustav's praise. We find there a lot of admiration for King's generosity, his noble deeds, commanders'

---

[72] Samuel Pufendorf, *Gesammelte Werke*, vol. 1: *Briefwechsel*, ed. Detlef Döring (Berlin: Akademie Verlag, 1996), 323, 326; Warmholtz, *Bibliotheca Historica*, part 9, 123.

[73] Pufendorf, *De rebus*, 3: § 80.

[74] Leo Braudy, *From Chivalry to Terrorism. War and the Changing Nature of Masculinity* (New York: Alfred A. Knopf, 2003), 148–149.

virtues and courage. Surely he could be another Lion of the North and support the Protestants' cause in whole Europe. However, when reading the story thoroughly, we will constantly encounter disturbing scenes, critical hints and derogatory remarks. Maybe all these expressions of admiration should be seen as a kind of compulsory lip service? Or maybe this feeling of confusion is due to the sheer size of the work, which consists of 600 pages in quarto, and was written during a long time? It is difficult to control such a vast material, so maybe the criticism is the outcome of the Author's lack of attention? But perhaps he knowingly "smuggled" some well-thought-out remarks of the King into the text which were not as positive as it might seem at first glance? The interventions of the censors were not significant, as they intended most of all to protect the concept of the absolute rule in the Kingdom of Sweden. Thus, some of the questions will remain unanswered.

Chapter III: Exotic encounters, forgotten tales

Among many dramatic events of the Northern War, the battle of Warsaw, which took place in the heat of the summer on 28th–30th July (New Style) 1656, is still being described and discussed. There is a number of reasons why the said event is so absorbing both for the historians and amateurs: this was a battle of daring manoeuvres and of exotic units, which used a variety of tactics and fought in difficult terrain. Many nations evoked later the memory of the struggle. August Riese believed that this was the battle "where banners of Prussia received the first laurel of glory" and the very name of "Brandenburg" was introduced to the history of the world.[1]

There are numerous books and articles on this fight, yet the work that in my opinion should occupy the first place is a book by Mirosław Nagielski *Warszawa 1656*, which constitutes an in-depth study of the battle based on the archival research and synthesis of earlier investigations.[2] For the English-speaking audience the best introduction to the circumstances of the fight is the description made by Robert I. Frost.[3]

In the summer of 1656 the situation was not beneficial to the Swedish side. Although King Charles Gustav was supported by the

---

[1] It must be admitted that this was a fairly late start. August Riese, *Die dreitägige Schlacht bei Warschau 28., 29. und 30 Juli 1656* (Breslau 1870), 2. The title page of this work bears the inscription: *Die Wiege Preussischer Kraft und Preussischer Siege* (*The Cradle of the Prussian Force and the Prussian Victories*).

[2] Mirosław Nagielski, *Warszawa 1656* (Warsaw: Bellona SA, 2009).

[3] Robert I. Frost, *The Northern Wars. War State and Society in Northeastern Europe, 1588–1721* (Harlow: Longman, 2000), 173–176.

new ally – the Elector of Brandenburg and his army, the guerrilla-war weakened the Swedes significantly. In contradistinction to the Poles, they suffered a great loss while replenishing depleted regiments.

The Polish-Lithuanian army consisted of about 40,000 soldiers, including the Tatars auxiliary forces of about 2,000 warriors. As it turned out later, during the fight, probably the main problem of the said army was its insufficient number of elite, heavy cavalry troops – hussars, which appears to be downright bizarre since the Polish-Lithuanian army was renowned for the abundance of horse and the skilled use of such troops in the battles. However, the long-term war destroyed the units which were most expensive to maintain – the heavy cavalry. The allied armies of Sweden and Brandenburg consisted of approximately 18,000 soldiers, and the greater part was the cavalry. R.I. Frost pointed out that in this engagement a certain reversal of the pattern operated: Swedes and Brandenburgians used their cavalry to conduct daring manoeuvres in the Eastern style of warfare, while the Poles tried to block them with the infantry and musket fire, implementing the tactics from the Western European theatre of war.

The shape of the terrain caused also a lot of difficulties for both sides. The Swedish-Brandenburg army approached from the North, along the right bank of the Vistula River. The soldiers, however, could move only through a narrow strip of land, which on the one side was restricted by the river and on the other by woods. The movements of the troops were also limited by wetlands and sand dunes near a small settlement of Praga – today one of the districts of Warsaw.

During the three-day battle the breakthrough came with two actions, both undertaken on the second day, i.e. on 29th July 1656. In the first one King Charles Gustav escaped from the aforementioned narrow passage while performing a difficult, wheeling manoeuvre. The second was the charge of the Polish hussars, who brought a lot of confusion in the ranks of the Swedish-Brandenburg troops, yet ended in defeat, for they received no support.

Although the Swedes and Brandenburgians were victorious, this success did not result in any strategic turn of the war. After losing the battle, the Polish-Lithuanian side recovered quickly and gathered dispersed troops. A Pufendorf's opinion is worth recalling:

> If there ever was a battle worth of memory, it was this one, with a predominant number of the enemy forces positioned in the convenient places. The glory of the victory must be attributed to the command of the King [of Sweden] and the bravery of both armies. However, the outcome depended substantially on fortune. [...] It was noted as something special that whenever the Swedish army turned, it was always accompanied by the wind blowing from behind, and the enemy faces were pelted by smoke and dust.[4]

The winged horsemen

The *husaria* phenomenon belongs to the most cherished among the historical legends of Poland and has been described so often that it would be possible to collect an entire library dedicated only to this formation.[5] And there are apparent reasons for such a fascination: the battles won, exotic look, or excellent horses. Movies, computer games and re-enactment groups contribute in our age to the preservation of this image.

The hussars as type of cavalry were not "invented" in the Kingdom of Poland but in Serbia and Hungary, where it served in fights against the Turks. Initially, it was a light horse equipped with large wooden shields and lances. These early hussars were used in Poland and Lithuania as support units for the heavy, late mediaeval cavalry. However, the Polish-Lithuanian hussars gradually began to use armour, and at the end of the sixteenth century the said units changed

---

[4] Pufendorf, *De rebus a Carolo Gustavo Sveciae Rege, gestis commentariorum libri septem, elegantissimis tabulis aeneis exornati cum triplici indice* (Nuremberg 1696), 3: § 27, trans. W.K.

[5] In my opinion the best guide to the issues regarding hussars is Zdzisław Żygulski's jun. *Husaria Polska* (Warszawa: Wydawnictwo "Pagina," 2000). See also Anna Wasilkowska, *Husaria. The Winged Horsemen* (Warszawa: Interpress, 1998) and Radosław Sikora, *Fenomen husarii* (Warszawa, Instytut Wydawniczy "Erica," 2013). However, for the English readers the best introduction should be *Polish Armies 1569–1696* by Richard Brzezinski and Angus McBride in popular Man-At-Arms Series of Osprey, no. 184 and 188, vol. 1 and 2 (London: Osprey Publishing, 1987).

into medium-heavy cavalry. But this does not mean that the hussars became sluggish and slow. The average hussar armour, used in the battle – not for the ceremony, weighed not more than 15 kilograms, which facilitated a fast ride.[6] Against the infantry, the hussars used 5-metre-long, but light, lances of aspen wood, hollow inside. They were also armed with long swords (*koncerz*), sabres, horseman's picks and pistols. At times hussars used also reflex bows. To this day a debate continues whether the hussars wore their wings in battles, and, if yes, whether these ornaments were attached to the armour or to the saddle. The wings acted as decoration and were borrowed from Turkish fashion – the elite troops in this country were sometimes marked with such a distinction. The hussars' armour was decorated with expensive furs of tigers, leopards and lynxes.

There were, of course, victories, such as the one near Kircholm in 1605, where much weaker Polish-Lithuanian forces wiped out the entire Swedish army. A decisive factor was the hussar's charge. According to Michael Roberts, "it was probably the most severe defeat ever experienced by the Swedish army."[7] In many other wars, for instance against Muscovy or Turkey, the *husaria* cavalry proved its value. Kłuszyn 1610, Chocim (Khotyn) 1621 and 1673 perpetuated the legend. The most remembered is of course the battle of Vienna in 1683.

Additionally, the cost of the formation of the hussar troops was tremendously high. Defeats in the wars with the Cossacks and Moscow prior to the Second Northern War led also to a great reduction in the number of the experienced hussars who were able to perform difficult manoeuvres. It has been estimated that during the said war with the Swedes, the formations of hussars amounted to no more than 7% of the total Polish-Lithuanian cavalry.[8] The guerrilla warfare

---

[6]   Żygulski jun., *Husaria Polska*, 49.

[7]   Michael Roberts, *The Early Vasas. A History of Sweden, 1523–1611* (Cambridge: Cambridge University Press, 1968), 403.

[8]   Jan Wimmer, "Materiały do zagadnienia liczebności i organizacji armii koronnej w latach 1655–1660," *Studia i Materiały do Historii Wojskowości*, no. 4 (1958): 493; Wiesław Majewski, "Wojna polsko-szwedzka 1655–1660 (potop)," in *Polskie tradycje wojskowe*, part 1, ed. Janusz Sikorski (Warszawa: Wydawnictwo Ministerstwa Obrony Narodowej, 1990), 300.

was conducted mainly by the light, Cossack-style horse. Only some of these units wore light armour in the form of chainmail and were called the *armoured* (Pl. *pancerni*). They constituted medium cavalry. Still, the conventional picture of the Second Northern War in Poland-Lithuania is dominated by heavily armoured hussars.

Recently the question of *husaria* as an efficient military formation has been raised by Robert I. Frost.[9] He protested against a simplified, romantic image of the winged horsemen presented by Peter Englund, who described them as the last mediaeval knights of Europe.[10] Frost believes that hussars as the formation were a good response to the geographical conditions of Eastern Europe but also to changes at the tactical and operational level induced by the early modern Military Revolution in tactics. Few years' service in the cavalry was also an important element of the education of a young nobleman and even some commoners had an opportunity to raise their status owing to a military career.

For the sake of our discussion, however, it is important to determine how the Swedes viewed hussars and other formations of the Polish-Lithuanian horse in the years 1655–1660. Would they support Frost's or Englund's opinions? Let us, therefore, ask Pufendorf for advice.

On 8th July 1655, just before entering Poland, the Field-Marshal Arvid Wittenberg summoned an officers' briefing. Only a few most important matters were on the agenda. "Wittenberg commanded that the officers should instruct the soldiers, mostly recruits, how to proceed in every single case. In particular they should not be swayed by loud clamour the Poles raised while attacking, but to expect them in the closed ranks. If they dispersed and scattered, that would result in destruction and there would be no rescue during the escape, because of the very fast Polish horses."[11] The cavalry of the enemy was

---

[9] Frost, *Northern Wars*, 16–19.
[10] Peter Englund, *Ofredsår. Om den svenska stormaktstiden och en man i dess mitt* (Stockholm: Atlantis, 1997), 32–46.
[11] Pufendorf, *De rebus*, 2: § 14.

also the major reason for concern, but there was no explicit note of *husaria*, only generally about the Polish horse.

However, the campaign proceeded very well, and soon the Swedes won victory after victory. On 3rd October (New Style) 1655 a major battle near Wojnicz took place.[12] It is believed that the said battle and the ensuing surrender of Krakow on 17th October constitute the end of the first phase of the Swedish war against Poland-Lithuania. The beginning of the encounter was not very successful for the Swedes. Colonel Bretlach, sent forward in the vanguard, got involved in a heavy fight. The rest of the Swedish army, in turn, could not come to his aid straight away due to a difficult road. In the next stage of the encounter, the Swedes were able to expand the ranks and push back the attacking light horse. This time the Swedes used the terrain obstacles to their advantage and succeeded in displacing 400 hussars from their position. It seems, however, that in the said struggle the hussars had an unusual, defensive task to fulfil – they had to be a stabilizing centre for the Polish forces.

After the defeat in the Wojnicz battle, the Polish army withdrew in disorder and besieged Kraków could not have any hope for help. Pufendorf points out that at Wojnicz: "the Swedes won 20 drums of the cavalry, many banners, including the banner of John Casimir and the entire supply carriages. They chased the fleeing for 5 miles. This victory was of great import for the king, because he saw that his soldiers started to get used to the Polish way of fighting, and that they prevailed over hussars, who had a terrible look in the battle."[13]

Yet, we may as well note a few encounters in which the *husaria* coped very well with the Swedish forces, especially with the cavalry. Very significant in this regard was the Polish victory in the Battle of Warka, fought on 7th April (New Style) 1656. Four months before the

---

[12] Wojciech Krawczuk, "Wojnicz w latach 1655–1660," in W. Krawczuk, P. Miodunka and K. Nabiałek, *Dzieje Wojnicza od XVI do XVIII wieku* (Wojnicz: Towarzystwo Przyjaciół Ziemi Wojnickiej, 2009), 275–283; Tadeusz Nowak, "Operacja krakowska 1655," in *Wojna polsko-szwedzka 1655-1660*, ed. Jan Wimmer (Warszawa: Wydawnictwo Ministerstwa Obrony Narodowej, 1973), 231–236.

[13] Pufendorf, *De rebus*, 2: § 28.

Battle of Warsaw a few banners of hussars supported by the light horse broke the Swedish *reiters* and dismounted the dragoons.[14] This engagement showed that the Swedes lacked experienced infantry and artillery. Pufendorf, in turn, held the commander of the Swedish troops, Margrave Friedrich von Baden, responsible for the said failure and accused him of too high confidence. "Although the number of Swedes was much smaller, they bravely persisted in a tight formation for two hours and killed several companies of Poles. However, they were overwhelmed by a sheer number of the enemy forces, [...]. Many of the newly raised troops were not yet familiar with the Polish way of fighting. They had, therefore, to resign and flee."[15] One of the Polish participants in this battle, Jakub Łoś, who served in the banner of medium cavalry – *pancerni*, wrote in his diary: "Our soldiers fought valiantly, especially the hussars, they broke the Swedish horse and set off in pursuit."[16] The experience from Warka could exert a considerable influence on the decisions taken during the Battle of Warsaw.

"Such an attack my eyes will never see again"[17]

The famous charge of the *husaria* carried out in the afternoon of the second day of the Warsaw battle, 29th July 1656, has been described by many historians. The latest, detailed study was prepared by Andrzej A. Majewski.[18] The action was performed in a desperate plight for the Polish-Lithuanian troops, in which the Swedes and Brandenburgians already conducted their wheeling manoeuvre and

---

[14] The best description of this battle is Paweł Skworoda's, *Warka–Gniezno 1656* (Warszawa: "Dom Wydawniczy Bellona," 2003), 134–144.

[15] Pufendorf, *De rebus*, 3: § 13.

[16] Jakub Łoś, *Pamiętnik towarzysza chorągwi pancernej*, ed. Romuald Śreniawa-Szypiowski (Warszawa: Wydawnictwo DiG, 2000), 66.

[17] Henryk Sienkiewicz, *The Deluge*, trans. J. Curtin, vol. II, chapter L (Boston: Little, Brown and Company, 1915), 597.

[18] Andrzej A Majewski, "Szarża husarska pod Warszawą 29 lipca 1656 roku," in *Przegląd Historyczno-Wojskowy*, no. 241 (2012): 167–174.

forced their enemies to reverse the front by 90 degrees. It seems that the hussars charge was a risky, not to say desperate, attempt to change a deteriorating situation. On the other hand, it could be considered beneficial for the attacking horse that the opposing Swedish forces, which were to take the brunt of the charge, consisted mainly of cavalry units, *reiters* of the Uppland and Småland regiments.

The reconstruction of the composition of the striking *husaria* unit is not a simple task. A. Majewski convincingly demonstrated that the charge involved Lithuanian banners, which numbered only about 340 hussars. It was ironic that the same Lithuanian hussars defected for a short time to Charles Gustav in late 1655.[19] Alexander Hilary Połubiński, Lithuanian field notary (*notarius campestris*), young but experienced commander led the attacking cavalry.[20]

When it comes to the literary description, no one has depicted this clash better than Henryk Sienkiewicz, who used many sources and historical publications to precisely present such a dramatic issue. Michał Wołodyjowski, one of the main characters in *Deluge*, portrayed the charge in the following way:

> The hussars gave rein to their horses. O God, what a sweep! They fell into the smoke, disappeared! My soldiers began to shout, "They will break them, they will break them!" For a while the hussars were invisible; then something thundered, and there was a sound as if in a thousand forges men were beating anvils with hammers. We look. Jesus! Mary! The elector's men are lying like stones on a street, like wheat through which a tempest has passed; and the hussars far away beyond, their streamers glittering. They are bearing down on the Swedes! They struck cavalry; the cavalry were down like a pavement! They struck a second regiment; they left that like a pavement! There was a roar, cannon were thundering; we saw them when the wind bore the smoke aside. They were smashing Swedish infantry. Everything was fleeing, rolling, opening; they went on as if over a highway. They had passed almost through the whole army, when they struck a regiment of the horse-guard, in which was Charles Gustav himself; and like a whirlwind they scattered the horse-guard.[21]

---

[19] The King of Sweden was openly enchanted by *husaria*. Nagielski, *Warszawa 1656*, 183.

[20] Although the name sounds peacefully and civilly, the *pisarz polny* was a high military officer. Henryk Lulewicz and Andrzej Rachuba, *Urzędnicy centralni i dostojnicy Wielkiego Księstwa Litewskiego XIV–XVIII wieku. Spisy* (Kórnik: Biblioteka Kórnicka, 1994), 108, 110.

[21] Sienkiewicz, *Deluge*, vol. II, chapter L, trans. by J. Curtin, 596–597, with some alterations by W.K.

At that very time an event occurred, which still remains ambiguous. And this is how Sienkiewicz saw the fight that took place during the final phase of the charge:

> Roch Kowalski rode up. He knew Charles Gustav, for he had seen him twice before. A horseman shielded the king; but those who were present said that lightning did not kill more quickly than Kowalski cut him in two. Then the king rushed at Pan Roch. [...] They rushed at each other so that the breasts of the horses struck. They raged. "I look," said the officer; "the king with his horse is on the ground." He freed himself, touched the trigger of his pistol, missed. The king's hat had fallen. Roch then made for the head of Charles Gustav, had his sword raised; the Swedes were weak from terror, for there was no time to save Charles, when Bogusław [Radziwiłł] rose as if from under the earth, fired into the very ear of Kowalski, broke his head and his helmet. [...] Zagłoba and I talked of what had happened. The man had served with the Radziwiłłs from years of youth; he considered them his masters, and at sight of Radziwiłł he was probably confused. Perhaps the thought had never come to his head to raise a hand on Radziwiłł.[22]

It is a dramatic, literary description. The popularity of Sienkiewicz's novel resulted in a symbolic grave of Roch Kowalski built near the road to the Church of our Lady of Loreto – the oldest church in the Praga district – with the inscription commemorating the brave knight.

The afore-mentioned description finds its confirmation in many contemporary sources. Various tales of a single hussar attacking the King of Sweden were collected by Adam Kersten and Mirosław Nagielski.[23] We shall recall a couple of them. A news pamphlet from Hague, printed in 1656, informs us briefly but succinctly about the incident.[24] We find there a detailed scene of the charge and attack on the King.[25] A piece of information that cannot be found elsewhere

---

[22] Sienkiewicz, *Deluge*, vol. II, trans. by J. Curtin, 597–598, with some alterations by W.K.

[23] Adam Kersten, *Sienkiewicz – Potop – Historia* (Warszawa: Państwowy Instytut Wydawniczy, 1974), 224; Nagielski, *Warszawa 1656*, 198–200.

[24] *Brief Pertinentelyck verhalende de effective Conjunctie van den Koningh van Sweeden Met den Kevr – Forst van Brandenburg Mitsgaders de Omstandicheden van het schrickelyk gevecht tusschen de selfde, ende de Polen, vorgevallen den 28.29 ende 30. Julii laestleden. Waer van de Victorie gebleven is by de voorschreve Protestante Princen. Geschreven uyt Warsaw den 4. Augusti. S'graven – Hage, by Adrian Vlacq MDCLVI*. It is available online in the resources of The Digital Library of Polish and Poland-Related News Pamphlets at: http://cbdu.id.uw.edu.pl/5370/ [4 June 2014].

[25] "De Houssaren / synde Polschen Adel met lancien seer wel ghemonteert / deden den eersten aenval op het Regiment van syne Majesteits Garde te voct / het welche vier stucken Ca-

(except for Sienkiewicz) reads as follows: the hussars were under fire coming from four cannons loaded with musket balls, positioned in front of the guard unit. According to this anonymous author, the King was attacked by one hussar with lance and wounded slightly in the right arm. Jakub Łoś, in turn, reports it in a different manner: "one servant attempted to attack the Swedish king. He ploughed his way through the soldiers and broke his lance. He would have achieved his ends, but for Prince Bogusław Radziwiłł who was faster with the pistol. The King Charles Gustav ordered to bury the dead knight solemnly. Our soldiers wondered: if only but a few of other units followed this banner of husaria, the Swede would not stand a chance to order the ranks."[26] And one more passage by Mikołaj Jemiołowski: "another brave cavalier reached the King with his lance, but the Prince of Prussia, who was present there with other officers, put him down. This hussar managed, however, to hit a Swede standing near with his lance and returned safe and sound."[27]

When describing the events occurring in the fog of the battle, it would seem that our knowledge of the charge and the attack on the King of Sweden is complete. However, at the end, we shall recall a Pufendorf's account. Will he confirm the afore-mentioned course of events?

> Meanwhile, all the forces of the enemy, except for a few squadrons that were with the infantry on a hill, surrounded the right wing of the King Charles Gustav to a large extent. Five thousand [!] hussars carried out a full force attack on the front of the Swedes. This big hit pressed two squadrons that too hastily shot from muskets. [Hussars] knocked many down, confused them, and stormed up to the second-line of troops. Yet they were received by the units of the second line and of the sides in such a way that only a few [hussars] were able to withdraw. And also those who fol-

---

nons met musketkogels geladen / vor en borstweer hadde / ende reusserden aenvancklich soo wel / dat de helst daer van door de de eerste gleder doorbrack / ende tusschen de selbe ende de troupen van reserve quamen te staen; maer d'ander helft dosr een Salve alte seer ghemcommodeert zynde / wierden sy alteghelyck / met het verlies van haeren Oberste ende seer veel dooden in desroute gheslagen. Up dese rescontre wierde syne Majesteit met een lancie / die hy met syn rapier parceerde / onder de rechter arm door syn kleedt gestooten [...]," *Brief Pertinentelyck*, 7.

26 Łoś, *Pamiętnik*, 70.

27 Mikołaj Jemiołowski, *Pamiętnik dzieje Polski zawierający (1648–1679)*, ed. Jan Dzięgielewski (Warszawa: Wydawnictwo DiG, 2000), 209.

lowed them were defeated, and some of those who then directed their attack on the infantry of the King and on the cavalry of the Elector were so harshly treated that they retreated back to the hill in disturbed ranks.

During these fights the Tatars tried to wheel around the village to attack the Swedish ranks from behind. Therefore, the King ordered four squadrons, under the command of his brother, to turn back and to head the approaching foe. [Tatars] were defeated, suffered a great loss of life [...].[28]

The above-mentioned description of the charge is consistent with the findings of modern historians, although the number of hussars was greatly overstated. The unit amounted not even to 500, let alone 5,000 soldiers. Such an exaggeration appears to be surprising in view of the next chapter in which Pufendorf gives a detailed and real overview of the Polish-Lithuanian army forces: "the enemy army consisted of eight thousand quarter soldiers, sixteen thousand nobles, five thousand Lithuanians, six thousand Tatars and four thousand infantry, although Poles proclaimed that their troops numbered a hundred thousand people, and because of the said number were sure of victory."[29] Let us see now how Pufendorf makes a threat to the King:

That day the life of the King was in grave danger. At about noon when the hussars and the Polish soldiers attacked from the hill the left wing of the Swedes, where the King stayed, six thousand Tartars struck the said wing from behind, near the village of Bródno. To repel the forces, the King led the regiment of the Elector's Foot Guards, along with some other troops, to deploy them in a convenient area. Meanwhile, a very fierce fight broke up, in which the King was so beleaguered with the enemy that he had no man nearby, only the captain of horse Trafvenfelt. He was surrounded by seven Tatars, armed with spears and argans.[30] The King shot at two warriors with his pistols and slashed the head of the third warrior, whose spear was entangled in the bridle of the royal steed, so hard with the sword that the Tatar fell off his horse. Then the King helped Trafvenfelt, who as well shot two Tatars, and fought with the rest of them. The other two fled. In this way the King saved himself from obvious danger.[31]

---

[28] Pufendorf, *De rebus*, 3: § 26.

[29] Pufendorf, *De rebus*, 3: § 27.

[30] In this passage Samuel Pufendorf used the Latin word *iaculus*. The *argan*, better known under the name *lasso* was a tether made of horse hair, used primarily by Tatars in herding, but also for capturing of the prisoners (*jasyr*).

[31] Pufendorf, *De rebus*, 3: § 26.

Beware – the Tatars are coming!

In the Polish historiography, there is a long-standing tradition of diminishing the importance of the military aid of the Tatars. Such an approach manifests itself clearly already in the writings of the "Father" of the Polish historians, Jan Długosz (1415–1480). Yet before we criticize such a stance, we shall point to circumstances that caused such an attitude.

We can find the origins of this ambivalence in the course of the Battle of Grunwald (Tannenberg) in 1410, one of the greatest battles of mediaeval Europe. The Polish-Lithuanian forces under the command of King Władysław Jagiełło defeated the knights of the Teutonic Order. There were also some Tatar units in the army of the Lithuanian Grand Duke Vytautas, which numbered most probably 1,000 warriors. The historians still dispute if the Tatars played a significant role in this battle, in so far as they simulated the flight and lured part of the Teutonic soldiers of the battlefield. Despite the large literature on this subject, the matter remains unresolved.

The use of these "pagan forces" helped later the Teutonic Order to launch a strong propaganda attack on the Polish-Lithuanian side.[32] The Order proclaimed the war not to be righteous, not *bellum iustum* owing to the participation of such units. The dispute continued at the Council of Constance (1414–1418), where the Poles had to refute these accusations. As a result, Długosz in his *Annales* decreased the number of Tatars participating in the battle to some 300 warriors. He as well assigned responsibility for the destruction of the Catholic churches in the Zawkrzański land to the said Tatars and Orthodox Lithuanians.[33]

In the seventeenth century the situation was not dissimilar. The Tatars were perceived in Poland-Lithuania as an implacable enemy, Ottoman Turkey's military arm, but sometimes as an ally likewise. It is worth recalling that we can distinguish two groups of Tatars: those

---

[32] Sven Ekdahl, *Grunwald 1410* (Kraków: Avalon, 2010), 115.
[33] Ekdahl, *Grunwald 1410*, 248–249.

from the Crimean Khanate and those living as citizens in the Grand Duchy of Lithuania already in the late Middle Ages, specifically since the end of the fourteenth century. These "home" Tatars served faithfully in the military units of the Lithuanian and Polish cavalry until the Second World War. Interestingly enough, they always kept faithful to the Muslim religion and prayed in mosques. That possibility of peaceful coexistence and cooperation of the followers of the two great religions: Christianity and Islam is only sporadically invoked.[34] In today's Poland and Lithuania we can still find a small group of Tatars, descendants of those mediaeval settlers.[35]

During the Second Northern War it was the Crimean Khanate that first assisted the Commonwealth with the military aid. Since 1654 this state was ruled by Khan Mehmed IV Giray Sufi, who was well disposed towards the Polish-Lithuanian Commonwealth, in witness whereof at the beginning of his rule he sent troops against the rebellious Cossacks and Russia. The society of Khanate was highly militarized, almost every man was an experienced warrior and a great horseman.[36] Sending a unit of some ten thousand braves did not present any difficulties as the Tartars specialized in high-speed and long-range campaigns.[37] But it must be remembered that the Tatar art of war and understanding of its purpose differed significantly from the

---

[34] Jurgita Šiaučiūnaitė-Verbickienė, "Tatarzy," in *Kultura Wielkiego Księstwa Litewskiego, analizy i obrazy*, trans. Beata Piasecka (Kraków: Universitas, 2011), 760–771; Jan Tyszkiewicz, *Tatarzy w Polsce i Europie. Fragmenty dziejów* (Pułtusk: Akademia Humanistyczna im. A. Gieysztora, 2008), 149–163. We should, however, add that some units of the Lithuanian Tatars joined the Swedes and remained in their service almost to the end of 1656. Wimmer, "Materiały do zagadnienia," 494.

[35] Two Tatar mosques in Bohoniki and Kruszyniany in Podlasie are still open and used for prayers. In Poland there are now about 3,000 Tatars.The basic criterion for belonging to the group is Islam and the tradition of origin. The Tatars are organized in Związek Tatarów Rzeczyspospolitej Polskiej (*Tatars Association of the Republic of Poland*) and Muzułmański Związek Religijny w Rzeczypospolitej Polskiej (*Muslim Religious Union in the Republic of Poland*).

[36] Bohdan Baranowski, "Tatarszczyzna wobec wojny polsko-szwedzkiej w latach 1655–1660," in *Polska w okresie drugiej wojny północnej 1655–1660* (Warszawa: Państwowe Wydawnictwo Naukowe, 1957), 453–489.

[37] Victor Ostapchuk, "Crimean Tatar Long-Range Campaigns: The View from Remmal Khoja's History of Sahib Gerey Khan," in *Warfare in Eastern Europe, 1500–1800*, ed. Brian L. Davies (Leiden–Boston: Brill, 2012), 147–171.

Swedish or Polish view on this matter. For the participants of such a raid it was above all an opportunity to get captives, which could be ransomed or sold on the Turkish market. The political or military objectives were less important and thus the Tatar contribution to the battles was often limited to the harassing of the enemy. However, we should not underestimate the psychological factor they caused, i.e. soldiers understood that slavery would be very hard to endure and therefore feared such an enemy. The events of 1656 confirmed the gravity of the said support.

From the very beginning of his reign Charles X Gustav considered the possibility of the Tatar intervention. The legation from Crimea, which appeared in Stockholm in May 1655, just before the start of the war, was very generously endowed. Khan decided, however, that he would aid the Commonwealth. In 1655 the Tatar troops appeared in Podolia and Ruthenia, blocking the action of the Cossacks, who could help the Swedes. King John Casimir encouraged the nobility to persevere, pointing to the expected arrival of the Tatars. The traitors could expect harsh punishment from the cruel warriors. In late 1655 the King of Sweden addressed the threat cautiously. He gave orders to General Robert Douglas to back off to the cities the moment he heard of the arrival of the Tatars, which the General instantly obeyed.[38]

Let us return now to the events of the Battle of Warsaw. Sources reveal active participation of the Tatars, even if historians still debate whether they played a major role in the said fight.[39] The sense of chaos Tatars brought concerning their contribution results most probably from their hit-and-run tactics. Nor can we forget their constant search for valuable captives, for whom they could charge a good price in Turkey. It is, therefore, likely that smaller and larger groups of exotic riders bustled in the battlefield. They did not constitute a grave threat to the troops of Sweden and Brandenburg, but could capture single cavalry – or infantrymen. We can, however, raise yet another

---

[38] Pufendorf, *De rebus*, 2: § 70.
[39] Wojciech Krawczuk, "O Rochu Kowalskim i Tatarach," in *Inter majestatem ac libertatem. Studia z dziejów nowożytnych dedykowane Profesorowi Kazimierzowi Przybosiowi*, ed. Jarosław Stolicki, Marek Ferenc and Janusz Dąbrowski (Kraków: Historia Iagellonica, 2010), 125.

question: why do almost all sources report only the hussars' attack on the Swedish king? Perhaps Pufendorf made a mistake relying on the account of Trafvenfelt.[40]

In explaining this intricate situation we can use the research carried out by Sławomir Augusiewicz regarding the Battle of Prostki, which took place on October 8th 1656.[41] The Swedish and Brandenburg troops lost the battle in which the Tatar units participated. As a consequence, Ducal Prussia was affected by the invasion, which was remembered until the Second World War. Prince Boguslav Radziwiłł was as well captured in the said battle. It was the Tatars who caught him, nonetheless, he was soon taken over by the Polish officers. The colonel Gabriel Wojniłłowicz, a relative of Radziwiłł, expressed a particular concern about such an important person.[42] Despite the Tatars' request, this valuable prisoner has not been returned into their hands. Moreover, a Polish envoy, sent later to Khan, had orders to deny that Tatars had captured the prince.[43] The aftermath of the Prostki battle shows clearly how effectively the Tatars acted while pursuing their prey.

In conclusion, we can state that in the second day of the Battle of Warsaw Charles Gustav was in serious danger. This is the only fact we can be sure of. There is every likelihood that the story of a brave hussar – a very compelling and dramatic one – was invented at the Polish court for reasons of wartime propaganda, for a story of a single knight fits much better to the legend of the battle than the action of some seven Muslim Tatars. The episode was probably added to the description of the *husaria* charge, which was and still is an undisputed evidence of the hussars' great courage. It is not as well immaterial that according to some stories, the traitor – Prince Bogusław Radziwiłł prevented the death of the Swedish King. This rumour

---

[40] Also Arne Stade voiced serious doubts on how to explain these vague stories about the attack on Charles Gustav. Arne Stade, *Erik Dahlbergh och Carl X Gustafs Krigshistoria. Carl X Gustaf Studier*, vol. 3 (Kristianstad: Militärhistoriska förlaget, 1967), 64, footnote 114.

[41] Sławomir Augusiewicz, *Działania militarne w Prusach Książęcych w latach 1656–1657* (Olsztyn: Ośrodek Badań Naukowych im. Wojciecha Kętrzyńskiego w Olsztynie, 1999), 72–89.

[42] Augusiewicz, *Działania militarne*, 110.

[43] Augusiewicz, *Działania militarne*, 111–112.

could be used against the Prince, and indeed such accusations were hurled after the war.[44] A few historians, to wit August Riese, suggest a possibility that the King of Sweden was attacked twice, first by a hussar, and later by the Tatars.[45] It seems, however, unlikely. We must accept the fact that the fog of the battle does not allow for a full assessment of the situation.

The Swedish horse

While describing the state of the Swedish army during the first year of the war with Poland-Lithuania, Lars Tersmeden drew our attention to the high proportion of cavalry, which amounted to more than a third of the entire force.[46] As for the description of the Swedish horse tactics, it is usually limited to information on the actions during the battles.[47] The *reiters* did not look as impressive as hussars, yet their effectiveness is worth examining. A prospect of a decisive battle, like the Battle of Warsaw, which could determine the fate of the conflict, still dominates in the studies into the Second Northern War. Although there were many battles fought in Poland-Lithuania in the years 1655–1660, the winning Swedes did not achieve any strategic success, while the losing Poles did not accept any defeat.[48]

Having read detailed descriptions of the campaigns in Pufendorf's *De rebus*, we gain some insight into the Swedish cavalry actions, which were by no means dominated by the battles. What is more,

---

[44] Nagielski, *Warszawa 1656*, 200.

[45] Riese, *Dreitägige Schlacht*, 142–143.

[46] At the beginning of the war the Swedish cavalry numbered 10,500, infantry 16,000, dragoons 650. Lars Tersmeden, "Carl X Gustafs armé 1654–1657. Styrka och dislocation," in *Carl X Gustafs armé. Carl X Gustaf Studier 8*, ed. Arne Stade (Kristianstad: Militärhistoriska förlaget, 1979), 197. Subsequent changes in the composition of the army indicate a further increase in the number of cavalry.

[47] Tersmeden, "Carl X Gustafs armé," 25–26.

[48] Jeremy Black, *Rethinking Military History* (New York: Routledge, 2008), 77.

it appears to be justifiable to claim that we can discern a consistent pattern of conduct that brought ample opportunities to the Swedes.

From the very beginning, after the first encounters, the Swedish commanders sent separate cavalry units for long raids. This, however, was a new tactic, a fruit of victories, for even in April 1655, before the start of operations, Charles Gustav ordered Field Marshal Arvid Wittenberg not to risk and not to disperse troops when entering Poland.[49] Nevertheless, after the surrender of the Polish levée en masse (*pospolite ruszenie*) in Ujście on 25th July 1655, Wittenberg sent forward a strong cavalry unit accompanied by Hieronim Radziejowski, Polish traitor supporting Charles Gustav. The goal was more political than military, Radziejowski had to convince his countrymen to submit to the Swedes.[50] It is the formula of sending forward a strong cavalry unit with an important errand, which repeats itself during the war in Poland. These actions should be analyzed more accurately, since they could, in fact, be as important as the battles.

After the battle of Żarnów on 16th September (New Style) 1655, "the King, in order to take advantage of his luck and not to leave the enemy any time to recover, decided to follow in the Poles' footsteps and found himself in the middle of their units. There was no question of a lack of success for this effort, because a mile from Kraków he approached the unsuspecting enemy so suddenly that he even overtook the messengers who had to report his arrival. The success could be greater: Swedish avant-garde, numbering eight hundred cavalry, and commanded by Colonel Bretlach, broke through the suburb and the burning buildings without encountering any resistance, reached the gates of the town, and found it open. There would be no trouble entering the town because the whole garrison took refuge in the castle. However, fearing an ambush, they withdrew and did not dare take advantage of such an opportunity."[51]

---

[49] Pufendorf, *De rebus*, 2: § 12, trans. W.K.
[50] Pufendorf, *De rebus*, 2: § 16, trans. W.K.; Adam Kersten, *Hieronim Radziejowski. Studium władzy i opozycji* (Warszawa: Państwowy Instytut Wydawniczy, 1988), 402.
[51] Pufendorf, *De rebus*, 2: § 27, trans. W.K. Adam Kersten does not confirm such a dramatic course of events, see Adam Kersten, *Stefan Czarniecki 1599–1665* (Warszawa: Wydawni-

The best example of an officer to whom these difficult tasks were entrusted, and who seized every opportunity given, was Rutger von Ascheberg. He drew on his extensive experience in long-range raids during the Thirty Years' War under the command of Gustavus Adolphus's generals. It was he who in the Winter of 1645 under orders from Field Marshall Lennart Torstenson marched into Austria with the vanguard of the Swedish army leading a unit of 130 reiters.[52] He described the event as the real beginning of his military career in his *Journal* published in 1951 by Alf Åberg. The manuscript of the *Journal*, which is a historical source of great value, (nonetheless, we have to separate boasts from real events), was as well quoted by Samuel Pufendorf.[53] Åberg believes that the actions prior to 1675 were described less accurate and they only list merits of Ascheberg's,[54] which does not reduce the importance of the said source – cavalry officers have always been prone to exaggeration.

Ascheberg with his detachment reached Poland in December 1655 after the beginning of the war operations and the first Swedish victories. Already on 28th January 1656 Charles Gustav deployed 240 reiters to perform a long range reconnaissance, from the town of Łowicz to Radom – a distance of 120 kilometres. Ascheberg was also to organize a repository for the approaching Swedish army. When the unit came to rest in a farm called Zakrzew, it was ambushed by 2,000 Poles. Among the attackers were professional soldiers but also peasants armed with scythes. They belonged to the Polish insurgent troops formed in this area by Stefan Czarniecki. Ascheberg managed to free himself from the trap. For Czarniecki the skirmish was a clear signal that he had to begin retreat, as his troops were inexperienced and unable to face the Swedish army under adverse conditions. It was

---

ctwo Ministerstwa Obrony Narodowej, 1963), 225. It was the same Colonel Bretlach who two weeks later was ambushed near Wojnicz.

[52] Hugo E. Uddgren, "Rutger von Ascheberg," in *Svenskt Biografiskt Lexikon*, vol. 2, ed. Bertil Boëthius (Stockholm: Albert Bonniers Förlag, 1920), 331–344.

[53] *Fältmarskalken Rutger von Ascheberg Journal och korrespondens till år 1680*, ed. Alf Åberg (Stockholm 1951), Kungl. Samfundet för utgifvande af handskrifter rörande Skandinaviens historia. Historiska handlingar del 34: 1.

[54] *Fältmarskalken Rutger von Ascheberg Journal*, 6.

the first such task for Ascheberg and he performed it with great bravery.[55] Since then we find a sequence of similar events in his reports. Already on 22nd February he was sent with a strong division ahead to secure the passage of the River San on the way to the town of Jarosław. He accomplished this task and conquered the town. When the situation deteriorated and the Swedish army was besieged, Ascheberg was deployed on 24th March with a strong unit in the direction of Kraków. This manoeuvre was to confuse the Poles and convince them that the Swedish army would seek refuge in this town.[56] On 5th April, after the Swedes managed to break the siege, Ascheberg was sent forward to protect the crossing on the River Wieprz. He gives accurate descriptions of these events, in contrast, the Battle of Warsaw has been presented in two sentences.

However, he paid special attention in his *Journal* to the clash fought on 24th December 1656 near Chojnice in Gdańsk Pomerania. He managed to seize Stefan Czarniecki, master of guerilla warfare, unawares. Czarniecki suffered great losses and was forced to change plans again. At the news of this victory, Charles Gustaw invited Ascheberg to his Royal table and bestowed generous gifts, upon him, such as a gold chain worth 2,000 Reichsthaler.[57]

The question arises how many such Aschebergs the Swedes had. In the first stage of the war they could use Polish troops, acquainted with the area, who joined Charles Gustav's side. Yet since spring 1656 such units were almost nonexistent. "Borrowed" from the East European theatre of war and applied by the Swedish army, long-range cavalry raids turned out to be a formidable concept.[58] The main problem

---

[55]   *Fältmarskalken Rutger von Ascheberg Journal*, 15–18, 192–194. Pufendorf, *De rebus*, 3: § 5. Jerzy Teodorczyk, "Wyprawa zimowa Czarnieckiego w 1656 r.," in *Wojna polsko-szwedzka 1655–1660* (Warszawa: Wydawnictwo Ministerstwa Obrony Narodowej, 1973), 279–281; Paweł Skworoda, *Warka–Gniezno 1656*, 90.

[56]   Stade, *Erik Dahlbergh*, 167, footnote 67.

[57]   *Fältmarskalken Rutger von Ascheberg Journal*, 23–26, 198–199; Jan Wimmer, "Przegląd operacji 1655–1660," in *Wojna polsko-szwedzka*, 178; Kersten, *Stefan Czarniecki*, 316–317. Since Poland-Lithuania applied the Gregorian calendar, the said clash has been described in the Polish monographs under the date of 3rd January 1657.

[58]   Brian L. Davis, "Introduction," in *Warfare in Eastern Europe, 1500–1800* (Leiden–Boston: Brill, 2012), 3–4, Jerzy Maroń, *Wokół teorii rewolucji militarnej. Wybrane problemy* (Wrocław: Wydawnictwo Uniwersytetu Wrocławskiego, 2011), 78–79.

the Swedes experienced was a lack of support from the local population. In case of failure they could not just scatter and disperse. The hit-and-run tactics employed by both sides still remains an interesting field of research.[59]

Conclusion

For many decades the conventional image of the Second Northern War in Poland was dominated by the following formula: quick-fire Swedish infantry versus unstoppable Polish-Lithuanian *husaria*. Consequently, descriptions of big and decisive battles evinced an avid interest. We find there a clear trace of "technological paradigm" of the twentieth century, requiring to devote special attention to modern weaponry and breakthrough actions.[60] The sheer fact that such encounters were rare was of no importance. In the Polish historiography we can as well discern an issue of insurrection against the Swedes and the guerrilla warfare. But again, this topic was also explained and exploited often in line with the current situation of Poland in the twentieth century.

While creating a synthesis of war, it is somewhat difficult to give due prominence skilfully to the issues relevant to the task undertaken, as we are dealing with a number of stereotypes, clichés, or emotions. Some themes, such as the import of the Tatars aid for the Commonwealth, are and have been reduced not only because of some aversion but also valid political reasons.

While examining the progress of war, we may notice a process of mutual learning of the enemies – the best example is the cavalry tactics of the long raids. In this aspect Pufendorf's *De rebus* is an

---

[59] Janusz Wojtasik, "Wojna szarpana Stefana Czarnieckiego w dobie potopu szwedzkiego (1655–1660)," in *Z dziejów stosunków Rzeczypospolitej Obojga Narodów ze Szwecją w XVII wieku*, ed. Mirosław Nagielski (Warszawa: Wydawnictwo DiG, 2007), 183–200.

[60] John Mosier, *The Blitzkrieg Myth. How Hitler and the Allies Misread the Strategic Realities of the World War II* (New York: Perennial, 2004), 7–18, 24.

excellent source of knowledge, since it is not "contaminated" by later concepts and theories of military historians and theorists. Further, it presents views that were nearly contemporary with the events described.

Chapter IV: The chanceries at war

During the summer of 1654 the relations between the Emperor and the King of Sweden exacerbated. The reason for the dispute was the status of the Town of Bremen in the Principality of Bremen, new acquisition of Sweden, where Field Marshall Hans Christoffer Königsmarck, an experienced general, was the Swedish province governor. The imperial chancery decided to express dissatisfaction in writing, therefore the secretaries of the Emperor prepared a special edict on the matter: "the very name of Königsmarck was listed there without any titles. Because of this disgraceful omission the King of Sweden commanded to reprove the imperial chancery. Königsmarck, with his usual courage, stated that he never feared the imperial cannons, thus he was not afraid of imperial paper and ink."[1]

Parallel to the war of soldiers and generals, yet another war was waged: the conflict of diplomacy pursued by the state chanceries. The great diplomatic congress in Münster and Osnabrück, which ended the Thirty Years' War in 1648, has been considered a new page in the history of diplomacy. A characteristic feature of the professionalization of diplomacy was the wider use of both ancient and new acts and privileges in the current political struggle. Accordingly, this required a thorough analysis and authentication of the sources.[2] Diplomats and historians working on the acts from the archives created a new branch of the research – the auxiliary sciences of history. The concept of *bella diplomatica* (*diplomatic wars*) was born. Equally important

---

[1]   Pufendorf, *De rebus a Carolo Gustavo Sveciae Rege, gestis commentariorum libri septem, elegantissimis tabulis aeneis exornati cum triplici indice* (Nuremberg, 1696), 1: § 19, trans. W.K.

[2]   Krzysztof Pomian, *Przeszłość jako przedmiot wiedzy* (Warszawa. Wydawnictwa Uniwersytetu Warszawskiego, 2010), 161–165, 459–461.

were the efforts of the administration to arouse appropriate and positive sentiments among the population towards the government – as Anna Maria Forssberg showed recently on the example of Sweden in the second half of the seventeenth century,[3] i.e. when the information began to flow faster and newspapers started to play a role similar to today's.

It is apparent that during writing of *De rebus*, Pufendorf was much more interested in the matters of diplomacy than in the description of military actions. The diplomatic intrigues, quarrels concerning the order of precedence, errors in the titles and the coat of arms on the seals were much more engaging for the *Historiographer Royal* than setting ranks in some battles. For us, however, it is almost *terra incognita*. Chapter by chapter, Pufendorf discusses the long-forgotten instructions for the ambassadors or envoys.

The profound knowledge of the structure and principles of the management of the administration of the early modern chanceries was imperative to describe the "war of documents." The question arises: how well versed was Pufendorf in this issue? What did he pay particular attention to? Before we try to answer these two questions, we should get acquainted with one of the more complex chancery systems of the time, i.e. of the Polish-Lithuanian Commonwealth.

The Office of the State

The organizational structure of the Polish-Lithuanian state chanceries was quite intricate, as it is reflected in the geopolitical reality of the great Commonwealth. It was also the result of a long evolution, which began in the fourteenth century. In the mid-seventeenth century two Polish Crown Chanceries and two Chanceries of the Grand Duchy of Lithuania existed. Basically, their responsibilities were the

---

[3] Anna Maria Forssberg, "Att hålla folket på got humor. Informationsspridning, krigspropaganda och mobilisering i Sverige 1655–1680" (Stockholm 2005), *Acta Universitatis Stockholmiensis. Stockholm Studies in History*, vol. 80.

same, the Polish chanceries were in charge of the Kingdom of Poland and Lithuanian chanceries of the Grand Duchy of Lithuania. The existence of two chanceries was justified by the need to maintain stability and continuity of the office activities – Chancellors and Vice-chancellors were often absent from the court, and it was the key issue to ensure that at least one chancery remained open. The geographical principle was crucial in the distribution of work. However, there was also a common area– Livonia: all the documents and letters for this province were to be issued under the seals of both chanceries: Polish and Lithuanian.[4]

In addition to these four main offices, there were also three smaller ones, incorporated into the larger chanceries. Two of them, the decree chanceries, were responsible for the judicial matters and handled royal courts; one was related to the Polish Crown chancery, and the other to the Lithuanian office. In 1569, as a result of the Diet and the Union of Lublin, when three Ukrainian palatinates were incorporated into the Kingdom of Poland, a new, Ruthenian chancery was created. It was responsible for the affairs of Ukraine and became an important part of the already existing Polish Crown Chanceries.[5]

A large number of secretaries stayed at the Royal Court, a number of whom were employed in the chanceries, many more were sent to different missions at home and abroad. In this way, using the king's secretaries, the central government could reach distant provinces of the Commonwealth.

There were two Chancellors – one Lithuanian and one Polish, and two Vice-chancellors for two parts of the state. In 1507 a new principle was introduced: when the Chancellor was secular, Vice-Chancellor was to be spiritual and vice versa. Not always, however, the King managed to choose a right person for such important posts. In 1650

---

[4]   *Volumina Legum*, vol. 2, ed. Jozafat Ohryzko (Petersburg 1859), 278; Wojciech Krawczuk, "The Sources on the Early Modern Livonia in the Polish Crown Chancery Books. The First Years of Sigismund III Vasa's Reign," in *Latvijas Vēstures Institūta Žurnālis*, no. 83 (2012): 89–97.

[5]   Petro Kulakovs'kyj, *Kanceluriju ruśkuj (wołyńskuj) Metrykł 1569–1683 rr. Studija z istoru ukraińskogo regionalizmu w Reczi Pospolitij* (Ostrog–Lwiw, 2002).

a magnate, Hieronim Radziejowski, was lifted to the Crown Vice-chancellorship. Quarrels and erratic behaviour in political matters led to his removal from the office already in 1652, when the threat of war was already looming, Radziejowski fled to Sweden and supported Charles Gustav during the invasion and the first stage of war. Eventually, he was accused of treason by the Swedes too. The allegations levelled were very similar to those previously made against him by the Poles.[6] Radziejowski epitomises a rebellious magnate holding a high office who did not pay any attention to the interest of the state.

The above-mentioned chanceries were not King's own but were considered as the offices of the Commonwealth. The King could of course influence their work, and his cooperation and decisions were necessary for the issuing of documents. On the other hand, the heads of offices – Chancellors and Vice-chancellors – saw themselves as guardians of the law, hence could refuse to seal any document beyond the laws of the Commonwealth. Such practices happened repeatedly and we can collect evidence of such objections, for example in the diaries of Albrycht Radziwiłł, Lithuanian Vice-chancellor and Chancellor in the years 1619–1656, to wit in 1633 Radziwiłł refused to seal the privilege for the Protestants stating that his conscience would not allow that.[7] The pressure from the King, who stressed that he would not sign an important proclamation, did not bring a desired effect. When in 1636, the King wanted to appoint some Germans as the forestry officers and to exclude them from previous jurisdiction, Radziwiłł refused to seal – disregarding the fact that the privileges were prepared – saying: "I treasure the law higher than the grace of the King."[8]

In the case of an honest and dedicated officer, a right to disobey the orders, even the King's orders, was a warranty of the maintenance of law. However, a powerful brawler and litigant who received the

---

[6] Pufendorf, *De Rebus*, 3: § 42; Adam Kersten, *Hieronim Radziejowski. Studium władzy i opozycji* (Warszawa: Państwowy Instytut Wydawniczy, 1988), 485–492.

[7] Albrycht Stanisław Radziwiłł, *Pamiętnik*, vol. 1, ed. and trans. Adam Przyboś and Roman Żelewski (Warszawa: Państwowy Instytut Wydawniczy, 1980), 301–302.

[8] Radziwiłł, *Pamiętnik*, vol. 1, 553.

offices of Vice-chancellor or Chancellor could seriously threaten the security of the state, and proclaim that their deeds were only intended to defend the existing laws.

The king's secret

The very concept of the *King's Secret* or *Secret du Roi* is generally associated with the eighteenth century and King Louis XV. He was the one who created a small, but efficient private chancery, whose primary task was to carry out the King's own foreign policy – which was often in conflict with the official policy of France.[9] Some historians believe that the French *King's Secret* together with the *Cabinet Noir* (the postal censorship) lay the foundation for today's Secret Services. However, such secret chanceries were not the French monopoly. They appeared in Europe long before the eighteenth century. Already in the Middle Ages some Royal chanceries implemented solutions that facilitated the influence of the King – such as the Privy Seal of England. Generally, the main trouble in researching such offices of the early modern age is a relatively small number of documents that remained. Often do we learn of their existence from the reports of the opposing party. Typically, only a few, trusted secretaries worked there – a subsequent serious problem pertaining to the identification of the staff.

Since the mid-sixteenth century the state of affairs in Poland-Lithuania favoured the creation of a chancery that would be dependent only on the King. After the fall of the Jagiellon dynasty in 1572, the Royal elections became part of the state laws. However, the position of an elected king was relatively weak, and central offices became a battlefield for influence of different factions. The creation of the King's own chancery could allow the monarch to conduct different political actions regardless of the Chancellors and Vice-chancellors,

---

[9]   Gilles Perrault, *Le Secret du Roi. Premiére partie: La passion polonaise* (Paris: Fayard, 1992).

who could oppose and organize some counter-charges. Initial studies on this issue show that in relation to Poland-Lithuania there was no place for a completely secret and hidden office. The process can be assessed rather as the transformation of the legal, private chancery of the King, which intervened more frequently in the field reserved for the offices of the state.

Recently Waldemar Chorążyczewski have undertaken studies on the earliest period of the existence of this chancery, i.e. the mid-sixteenth century.[10] The main task of the king's private chancery, called also cabinet or chamber chancery, was to handle monarch's personal affairs, which was perfectly legal. But at the end of the rule of the last Jagiellon, Sigismund II Agustus (1520–1572), it turned out that it was a very convenient tool for influencing internal and external affairs of the state, for the King did not have to negotiate with the ministers, was not afraid of their opposition, could expedite his actions and conduct his own foreign policy. In the King's private chancery only a few secretaries and notaries worked who ensured the maintenance of secrecy. Chorążyczewski believes that it was 1567 that heralded the emergence of the cabinet chancery, when Stanislaus Fogelweder, the first private secretary of the King, was employed at the court. The King's secretaries were royal servants, therefore they did not have to swear an oath to uphold the laws of the Commonwealth, they were bound by an oath of fidelity only to the King. The creation of this office did not go unnoticed. From this time on in the parliamentary constitutions and royal commitments we will meet repeated bans: the King shall not use his private seal to the affairs of the state.[11]

The private chancery of the Polish kings gained immense importance during the reign of the Vasa dynasty in Poland-Lithuania

---

[10] Waldemar Chorążyczewski, "Początki kancelarii pokojowej za Jagiellonów," in *Polska kancelaria królewska. Między władzą a społeczeństwem*, part 3, ed. Waldemar Chorążyczewski and Wojciech Krawczuk (Warszawa: Wydawnictwo DiG, 2008), 33.

[11] "We promise with our Royal word that we and our descendants will not use any signet or separate (private) seal in the affairs of the Commonwealth, both in and outside the Kingdom, only these (seals) which are at the Chancellors and Vice-chancellors." *Volumina Legum*, vol. II, 152, trans. W.K. This obligation of King Henri Valois was repeated by his successors, yet it was not observed.

(1587–1668). It is evidenced by a sheer number of seals on the documents. We know 52 different Royal seals of the period, and as many as 19 are private chamber seals of the kings from the House of Vasa.[12] These signet rings and seals were pressed both on the ruler's private letters and state documents. Additionally, private seals of the monarch enjoyed recognition and gradual acceptance among state officers and nobility. Officially, those private seals were of much need – for example at a time when there was no Chancellor or Vice-chancellor present at the court and the chancery had to seal urgent dispatches. In 1632 during the session of the parliament, Adam Kazanowski advised officers that the King's private seal could only be used for minor matters of the state.[13] Yet, such proceedings were always treated with suspicion.

As it turned out, the fears were not unfounded. In 1646 King Władysław IV Vasa called on the restless Cossacks to the war with Turkey by sending them letters stamped with his private seal. The ensuing, official abolition of the said letters deemed illegal caused great outrage and helped Bohdan Khmelnytsky to incite the great Cossack revolt in 1648. As observed by Henryk Litwin, the ill-considered decisions of Władysław IV Vasa contributed heavily to utter annoyance of the Cossacks.[14] Thus, one of the biggest disasters that ever happened to the Commonwealth was due to the unlawful activities of the private chancery of the monarch.

The materials presented by Pufendorf show clearly that also during the reign of John Casimir Vasa, the monarch's private chancery did not lose its importance, especially when it comes to the matters of international politics. In the year 1654 Swedish diplomatic agent Johan Kock arrived in Warsaw. Kock had orders to investigate the state of affairs in Poland-Lithuania, and to gather all the important information about the enemy. Pufendorf contained in *De rebus…*

---

[12] Wojciech Krawczuk, "Kancelaria pokojowa za Wazów," in *Polska kancelaria królewska. Między władzą a społeczeństwem*, part 3 (Warszawa: Wydawnictwo DiG, 2008): 50.

[13] Radziwiłł, *Pamiętnik*, vol. 1, 230.

[14] See the statement of Henryk Litwin in *Polska na tle Europy XVI–XVII wieku. Konferencja Muzeum Historii Polski 23–24 października 2006* (Warszawa 2007), 109.

a list of issues Kock had to resolve. It was also both a diplomatic and a spy mission, with an emphasis on the latter.[15] The talks were difficult, the sides argued, inter alia, about chancery matters, the language of documents, titles and seals. John Casimir decided then to address Charles Gustav in French, as he did towards Queen Christina. Kock refused to accept it, since he was ordered to receive letters in Latin only. "Irrespective of what Christina did, Latin was once the language used between kings and senators of both kingdoms, and it was appropriate for negotiations. The case was certainly the public one."[16] The representative of the Polish side responded: "this is a new demand, difficult to reconcile with the Treaties. Letters that were issued in the King's chamber should not be written exactly in compliance with the pacts and should be treated more like private than public letters." Kock addressed these objections: "The difference between the King's chamber and the chancery is irrelevant. The importance of the answer (that Swedes demanded) exceeds by far private matters."[17] In this brief exchange of words we get the confirmation of the existence of two centres of foreign policy of Poland-Lithuania. One of them were the complex chanceries of the state, divided and difficult to operate. The second centre was a small group of close associates of the King working in the chamber chancery.

At this early stage of conflict all the chanceries could not boast about their achievements. A semi-official diplomatic mission of King John Casimir's messenger, Henri de Canasilles, to Sweden in 1654 turned out to be a total failure. Canasilles, the treasurer of the Polish queen and secretary of the King, was a counterpart of agent Kock, his mission involved sensing the mood in Sweden. An attempt to disrupt

---

[15] Pufendorf, *De Rebus*, 1: § 44; Józef Włodarski, Roman Makutonowicz, "Wywiadowcza penetracja Prus Królewskich i Korony przez Szwedów w latach 1652–1655," in *Komunikacja i komunikowanie w dawnej Polsce*, ed. Krzysztof Stępnik and Maciej Rajewski (Lublin: Wydawnictwo Uniwersytetu Marii Curie-Skłodowskiej, 2008), 83–94.

[16] Pufendorf, *De Rebus*, 1: § 45, trans. W.K.

[17] Pufendorf, *De Rebus*, 1: § 45, trans. W.K.

Charles Gustav's accession to the throne brought about only further exacerbation and gave the Swedes a new reason for war.[18]

However, in the following years, the chamber chancery of John Casimir proved its usefulness. Another secretary of the king, named Trabuc, achieved considerable and positive results in playing an intricate diplomatic game in 1658. It is no accident that most private secretaries of the Polish King were French. The Queen herself, Louise Marie from the House of Gonzaga, took care of it. In this way she could easier conduct the affairs with the French court at Versailles. Trabuc, acting incognito, and pretending to be a French diplomat, played a decisive role during the negotiations on the submission of the town of Toruń (Thorn) to the Swedes. According to the observers, these very negotiations opened a way to the Peace Congress in Oliva, which ended with peace settlement in 1660.[19]

Even before the talks in Oliva, the chamber chancery tried hard to prove its worth. One of the main points of the dynastic conflict was the use of Swedish coats of arms by King John Casimir. The Polish side, wishing to avoid a dispute before the negotiations, decided to create a new seal with an emblem presenting the Lithuanian Chaser (*Pogoń*) carrying a coat of arms of the Kingdom of Sweden on the shield that covered his chest. It was the King's personal seal, to which the Swedes objected at once. They did not approve documents sealed with this new sigil indicating that "in such cases they [the Poles] should use the seal of the Kingdom [of Poland]."[20]

The research on the private chanceries of the Vasa dynasty is in its initial phase. Nonetheless, it is definite that the findings in this field can substantially change our understanding of the early modern Polish-Lithuanian diplomacy.[21]

---

[18]   Robert I. Frost, *After the Deluge. Poland – Lithuania and the Second Northern War 1655-1660* (Cambridge: Cambridge University Press, 1993), 37–39.

[19]   Pufendorf, *De Rebus*, 3: § 58.

[20]   Pudendorf, *De Rebus*, 6: § 75, trans. W.K.

[21]   Krawczuk, *Kancelaria pokojowa*, 47–54.

The seals and titles

In the mid-seventeenth century a meticulous analysis of the form and content of the documents constituted the first step in the opening of any diplomatic negotiations.[22] The secretaries tried to recognize the mistakes, hence question the validity of the acts. It did not result from viciousness but acted as a valuable asset enabling the achievement of superiority at the beginning of talks. Today, psychologists point out that at the start of negotiations predominance of one party could be determined on the basis of trivia. Early modern diplomats also possessed the knowledge on that matter. They understood well all the arcane of the game, and sometimes, when there were more important matters at stake, they suspended such niceties. In 1654 when the agent Kock was sent to Poland, he received the following instruction from his Swedish principals: "if in the submitted documents the title of the King of Poland is correct, Kock has to accept the acts. He should not have to worry about the seal, but pretend that he has not noticed it."[23] The problem concerned the coats of arms of Sweden placed permanently on the Polish and Lithuanian seals, at times the Swedish side was willing to make concessions and forget the issue for a moment. In 1656, when the preparatory phase of negotiations between the Commonwealth and Sweden was launched, King John Casimir stated: "he would rather lead them secretly and without any ceremony, so that the commissioners did not have to discuss the subtleties of power and formulas, but proceed with the case without undue intricacies to examine and sort out the main points of disagreement, which then could be agreed in a suitable form and signed in the official meeting."[24]

---

[22] This section is based mainly on: Wojciech Krawczuk, "Uwagi Samuela Pufendorfa o praktykach kancelaryjnych w XVII wieku," in *Polska kancelaria królewska. Między władzą a społeczeństwem*, part 4, ed. Waldemar Chorążyczewski and Wojciech Krawczuk (Warszawa: Wydawnictwo DiG, 2011), 107–115.

[23] Pufendorf, *De Rebus*, 1: § 44, trans. W.K.

[24] Pufendorf, *De Rebus*, 1: § 58, trans. W.K.

The importance of the form of the document, however, was not limited only to the diplomatic game. In this way, the rulers could express their claims. The whole document served as the emanation of monarch's dignity, thus it had to be respected. Such an approach was especially characteristic of the diplomacy of the Russian tsar. By contrast, Dutch chanceries did not care at all what documents looked like.[25] In 1657 Charles Gustav received a caustic letter from States-Generals of the Netherlands, in which a States title was placed prior to the King's name, the paper, in turn, was full of blots. The King ordered to send the letter back and did not address Dutch diplomats.[26] Admittedly, the diplomats of the Netherlands had a very pragmatic approach to diplomacy, sometimes sparking outrage. During the negotiations in 1656, when the common cause of the Protestants was discussed, which could undeniably suffer from the proceedings of the Dutch, they "rejected it with laughter, mocking that their evangelical case was trade and well stuffed pouch."[27]

In a similar, meticulous manner the Swedes studied the documents of the Danish envoys. But sometimes they met their match.[28] When they contested Danish commission, because it was written on paper and not on parchment, the Dane, Oluf Pasberg countered promptly: "but parchment is usually bleached by lime, which eventually destroys letters!" The Swedes answer remains unknown.

We can notice obvious reluctance towards the republics of England, Netherlands and Venice. In 1654 the Elector of Brandenburg demanded from the King Charles Gustav that: "his deputy in Sweden should be treated in the same way as the Venetian and Dutch envoys. Recently the Swedes did not agree to settle this matter in Lübeck, they wanted to consent to the title of "Excellency" and a decent place

---

[25] We may wonder whether such criticism did not result from the aversion of Pufendorf to the republican system of government, or the poor condition of Dutch diplomacy at the time confirmed by the research of Martinus A.M. Franken, "The General Tendencies and Structural Aspects of the Foreign Policy and Diplomacy of the Dutch Republic in the Latter Half of the 17th Century," in *Acta Historiae Nerlandica*, vol. 3 (1968): 19–21.

[26] Pufendorf, *De Rebus*, 4: § 95, trans. W.K.

[27] Pufendorf, *De Rebus*, 3: § 94, trans. W.K.

[28] Pufendorf, *De Rebus*, 6: § 46, trans. W.K.

only for the head of the diplomatic mission [from Brandenburg], yet, the Swedes conferred equal status to all three diplomats of the Netherlands. It would be appropriate that the King treated the envoys of Monarchs better than the envoys of the republics, because of the common system of government."[29]

Such niceties occupied the chanceries also in the moments of deepest crisis. In the year 1654, when it was still possible to prevent the war, the Polish Chancellor, while talking to Kock – Swedish diplomatic agent, raised some concerns: "that the title of Charles Gustav was placed prior to the title of the King of Poland – because when all the other kings: of Spain, France, England and Denmark, were preparing letters to the King of Poland, they always started them not with their names and titles, but with titles of the Polish King. The Chancellor would also prefer the use of the title 'His Majesty' in regard to the King of Poland instead of the 'Serene Enlightened,' since the Kings of Spain, France and Poland used 'His Majesty' when writing to each other, and for this purpose the Polish King used his great seal which depicted the figure of his majesty."[30]

Among the reasons for issuing a declaration of war in the early modern age, we will also find points relating to the practices of the chanceries. The justification of the attack on Poland-Lithuania was being prepared in Moscow for many years. Already in 1650 the Russians demanded severe punishment for perpetrators who committed irregularities in the use of tsar's titles.[31] Pufendorf notes that among the reasons for declaring war against Poland-Lithuania in 1654 the Russians indicated that the Poles failed to gild one letter in the tsar's name.[32] Thus, any changes of the tsar's titles were monitored with great concern. In 1655 the Russians showed their great discontent because the tsar was not granted new titles by the Swedes. The Swedish envoy managed to get out of trouble playing sharp: "The Russians

---

[29] Pufendorf, *De Rebus*, 1: § 12, trans. W.K.
[30] Pufendorf, *De Rebus*, 1: § 45, trans. W.K.
[31] Janusz Dąbrowski, *Senat koronny. Stan sejmujący w czasach Jana Kazimierza* (Kraków: Historia Iagellonica, 2000), 64–65.
[32] Pufendorf, *De Rebus*, 3: § 47.

will not accept letters without new titles? In that case, the Swedes will no longer write to them."[33] A special attention to the form of documents was characteristic of the Moscow grand ducal chancery already in the sixteenth century.[34]

Further, Russian diplomacy tended to treat envoys almost like prisoners. They could not move freely around Moscow and were held in detention. "When the Swedish envoys complained that their servants could not go to the town, the Russian Chancellor, who was a deputy in Stockholm in 1649 said that Axel Oxenstierna told him then: When travelling to a foreign country, you should not bring your habits, but accept those existing in the very place."[35] With the growing hostility it could be easily seen that the war was approaching.

> Every year, at the beginning of their fasting, the Russians reviled Lutherans, calling them heretics and pagan dogs. Those Swedes who came to Moscow for the conduct of trade were exposed to a variety of unpleasant, sometimes ugly insults, thrown at them as if they were dogs, and when they complained to the authorities, they were still mocked. When it happened that one of our Swedes killed one Muscovite, it was proclaimed in the place of execution that this heretic and infidel killed a Christian, and therefore he had to die. These and many other signs showed that de la Gardie knew that Muscovites had no friendly feelings.[36]

Officially, the cause of the Second Northern War between Sweden and the Polish-Lithuanian Commonwealth was the pretence of King John Casimir, who made a claim to the Swedish crown, and referred to the dynastic rights of the Polish Vasas. This claim was expressed by his titles and coat of arms. The code was simple and clear for the recipients of letters and documents, therefore, secretaries had to pay attention to all the changes in the messages, concessions and new additions. Three open crowns and a lion on the seal of the Polish King were a horror and usurpation for the Swedish officials.

---

[33]   Pufendorf, *De Rebus*, 2: § 77, trans. W.K.
[34]   Waldemar Chorążyczewski, Agnieszka Rosa, "Samoświadectwa pracowników polskiej kancelarii królewskiej czasów nowożytnych. Przypadek sekretarza królewskiego Jana Piotrowskiego," in *Polska kancelaria królewska. Między władzą a społeczeństwem*, part 4 (Warszawa: Wydawnictwo DiG, 2008), 97.
[35]   Pufendorf, *De Rebus*, 3: § 78, trans. W.K.
[36]   Pufendorf, *De Rebus*, 3: § 77, trans. W.K.

The Polish answer, written in the following month, was taken to Sweden by Jerome Zaworski. He delivered it to Stockholm in June, but except for the letter to the Council (of the Kingdom of Sweden), he did not have anything to prove the credibility of his public mission – but the passport. He proved it, although nobody demanded it, and the Polish King had the title of the King of Sweden in the said letter. The submission of this document was unnecessary, since Zaworski sailed directly by the sea from Gdańsk and did not travel by some foreign countries, for which he was reprimanded.[37]

All the parties involved, however, were well aware that the coat of arms and titles were but a veil covering the real causes of the conflict: economic, geopolitical and military. We shall recall here the speech of the Polish envoy Przyjemski, who, in an attempt to stop the Swedish army, pointed out that even if any errors occurred in the Crown chancery, they should not be avenged by the war.[38]

The secretaries had to be cautious about the changes of other forms of address, e.g. those referring to the legal status of the cities in the Holy Empire. In the year 1654 the great anxiety of Swedes aroused because of the term *Reichstadt* allegedly used by the Emperor's Chancery in relation to the town of Bremen, which remained under the rule of the King of Sweden.[39] Attempts to the liberation of the town from the Swedish domination ended then with a bloody conflict.

The chancery clerks examined carefully the way in which seals were affixed to documents. In 1655 they noted that in the letters from the tsar to Charles Gustav the Russian signet was attached so that the title of the Swedish king was bent, as if under the weight of tsar's seal. The Swedes interpreted this unambiguously – the tsar wanted to show who was the subject to whom.[40]

Another important issue was to ensure that no other country enjoyed a priority of the seals used when signing some treaties. During negotiations with the English in 1656 the Swedish envoy, Julius Coyet, had to pretend that the final document was sealed properly. "Since

---

[37] Pufendorf, *De Rebus*, 2: § 3, trans. W.K.
[38] Pufendorf, *De Rebus*, 2: § 21.
[39] Pufendorf, *De Rebus*, 1: § 21. See also: Björn Asker, *Karl X Gustav: en biografi* (Lund: Historiska Media, 2009, 2nd edition 2010), 173.
[40] Pufendorf, *De Rebus*, 1: § 77.

Rosenvinge, Danish minister, refused to agree that an agreement between Denmark and the Protector was sealed with the smaller seal, but demanded a large one, then also Coyet had to secure the same seal."[41]

Still other rules were used by Ottoman diplomacy. It appears that it paid careful attention to the essence of the matter and was not always interested in the issues of the protocol. A good example is the legation of Mustafa Aga: "he was an envoy sent [in 1656] by the Sultan of Turkey to John Casimir. When he saw a change of situation in Poland, he asked: is King John Casimir still in the kingdom? When he received a negative reply, he stated: his orders relate to the Polish king, so he decided to go to Charles Gustav, as the Polish crown remains in his hands. They [the Turks] have such habits: if someone was sent from the Ottoman court to another ruler, and this one died at that time, or other change took place, the envoy was required to continue his mission at the successor."[42] The Swedes were impressed but the negotiations soon collapsed due to a lack of proper credentials. Prince Rákóczy of Transylvania based his plan on similar reasoning, when, against the will of the Sultan, he undertook military cooperation with Sweden: "he believed that the Turk would not oppose, since the matter had already been raised, and the fate favoured the project. This [Turkish] nation was in fact used to evaluate all the events in reference to the result."[43] Actually, Rákóczy was not wrong – after a total defeat in Poland, he fell into disgrace at the Turkish court.

The Swedes documented exotic customs and behaviour of Turkish diplomats and courtiers with great interest. Pufendorf devoted a few chapters to the Swedish mission in Constantinople in 1657 – as he did not use the name Istanbul.[44] One illustration in *De rebus...* presents Great Audience given by Charles Gustav to Mustafa Aga (Hanassa) in the castle of Działdowo (Soldau) in 1656. And the Nordiska Museet in Stockholm stores a collection of thirteen paintings, commissioned by a Swedish diplomat Claes Rålamb, representing

---

[41] Pufendorf, *De Rebus*, 2: § 86, trans. W.K.
[42] Pufendorf, *De Rebus*, 2: § 95, trans. W.K.
[43] Pufendorf, *De Rebus*, 4: § 9, trans. W.K.
[44] Pufendorf, *De Rebus*, 4: § 23, 24.

the solemn departure of Sultan Mehmed IV, leaving the capital for a hunting expedition in 1657.

Swedish diplomats collected rumours circulating in Constantinople. "The success of King Charles Gustav in Poland aroused a lot of anxiety among the Turks, because of the old prophecy that the Ottoman Empire would be destroyed by people with golden hair.[45] Supposedly, it was to justify the failure of their diplomatic mission.

The *Seven Books* are full of descriptions of diplomatic meetings at the highest possible levels, of the disputes concerning the precedence of the diplomatic carriages and different ceremonies. This is the world of Baroque, full of pomp and much different from our reality. However, we may sometimes be surprised when it comes to the show of wealth and power. In June 1657 Swedish envoy Gustaf Lilliecrona arrived with a mission to Bohdan Khmelnytsky – Ukraine's factual ruler. He found Hetman in Czehryń: "Khmelnytsky received him in an informal manner and in poor condition. The room in which Lilliecrona addressed the audience served [Khmelnytsky] also as a dining room and a bedroom, and his family dwelled there too."[46] The Swede recorded it in disgust, however, for us it is an important clue that free Cossacks did not pay much attention to symbols and glamour of power, and their leader enjoyed the authority and respect regardless of the external decorum.

The language as well played a considerable role. In the mid-seventeenth century Latin was gradually supplanted by French as the language of diplomacy. Some courts, such as the Imperial, preferred German, so as not to give satisfaction to the French opponents. Although Queen Christina Vasa was an advocate of the use of French, arguing that it confirmed the close relationships between the kingdoms, Swedish Royal Chancery strongly insisted on the use of Latin.[47] This caused significant problems, especially in diplomatic rela-

---

[45] Pufendorf, *De Rebus*, 4: § 23.
[46] Pufendorf, *De Rebus*, 4: § 27, trans. W.K.
[47] Sven Ingemar Oloffson, *Efter Westfaliska Freden. Sveriges yttre politik 1650–1654* (Stockholm, Kungl. Vitterhets Historie och Antikvitets Akademiska Handlingar, Historiska Serien 4, 1957), 100–103, 105.

tions with the Dutch and the English, who could not find suitable translators.[48] The choice of Latin was, however, in the case of Sweden, quite rational, because of the political indifference of this language. It belonged to everyone and was not a "property" of any country. References to antiquity were also welcome. The Kingdom of Sweden pursued a very active policy when it comes to the construction of the image of its "ancient" history. This new European power was presented as the Kingdom of the Goths and Vandals, who destroyed imperial Rome. For this purpose the Swedish state financed also antiquarian work to document its past heroic achievements.[49]

The postal issues

As it has been newly indicated by Magnus Linnarsson, the Thirty Years' War had a positive influence on the development of the postal system, especially this of Sweden.[50] The extension of military operations over the large areas required more effective lines of communication. In the following years the importance of the efficient post increased, not only because of the rapid development of the instruments of diplomacy during peace negotiations, but also on account of the preparations for the new wars. Across Europe a new system of exchange of information was developed in the form of newspapers, which could quickly reach the recipient.

This does not mean, however, that the flow of information via post went uninterrupted through unfriendly external actions. The security of dispatched messages was particularly important during the diplomatic negotiations, and Pufendorf noted such issues with due

---

[48]   Pufendorf, *De Rebus*, 1: § 34, 3: § 70.

[49]   Johanna Widenberg, *Fäderneslandets antikviteter. Etnoterritoriella historiebruk och integrationssträvanden i den svenska stormaktstidens antikvariska verksamhet ca 1600–1720* (Uppsala 2006. Studia Historica Upsaliensa 225).

[50]   Magnus Linnarsson, "The Development of Swedish Post Office," in *Connecting the Baltic Area. The Swedish Postal System in the Seventeenth Century*, ed. Heiko Droste (Stockholm: Södertorns högskola, 2011), 26–27.

details. A good example is the description of the great crisis of 1657, which occurred in relations between Sweden and the Netherlands, when the Swedish postal messenger was robbed on the vital route from Hamburg to Stockholm.

> The Danes, shortly before they started the war, intercepted some letters, which were sent via Hamburg to Stockholm. Among other things, they found the letter of [a Swedish diplomatic agent] Appelbom to the Swedish Council of the Realm. They opened the said letters, added something here and there, translated them into Dutch and then handed them over to Dutch envoys residing in Copenhagen. They, in turn, sent the scripts to Hague, where they were later published. When these were read at the meeting of the States-General, it caused a great uproar, and the Dutch were especially offended by the words of Appelbom: If only he had had enough money, he could have won a lot of friends here, and it would be a considerable aid for the Swedish case, because both a Dane and a Spaniard had already bribed many.[51]

In such circumstances the diplomatic crisis could only be settled with great difficulty. However, the illicit access to the information was too important to give it up because of some diplomatic agreements. This way of thinking appeared very clearly during the preparations for the Peace Conference in Oliva in 1659: "The letters of the Swedes were intercepted and after deciphering they were made public. When the Swedes complained, the allies mocked that they ensured the safety of such letters, which were carried by special couriers and not by public post."[52] We can include such actions on account of the early modern intelligence, and stress that in the context of the Northern War this topic remains as well unexplored.[53]

---

[51]   Pufendorf, *De Rebus*, 4: § 93, trans. W.K.
[52]   Pufendorf, *De Rebus*, 6: § 77, trans. W.K.
[53]   Józef Włodarski and Roman Makutonowicz, *Wywiadowcza penetracja*, 83–94; Heiko Droste, *Schwedische Korrespondenz über Polen am Beispiel Heinrich von Schöllens, Kommissar in Breslau von 1664–1666*, in *Po obu stronach Bałtyku. Wzajemne relacje między Skandynawią a Europą Środkową. On the Opposite Sides of the Baltic Sea. Relations between Scandinavian and Central European Countries*, vol. 1, ed. Jan Harasimowicz et al. (Wrocław: Wydawnictwo "Via Nova," 2006), 121–130.

The battle of Ven

A very good example of a "battle of documents" is diplomatic struggle of the Swedes and Danes concerning the possession of the island of Ven (*Hven*) in 1658. This small island of 7,5 square kilometres lies in a strategic point in the middle of the Öresund Strait. It became known in the sixteenth century when the Danish astronomer Tycho de Brahe built two observatories there, and until the mid-seventeenth century it was the only reason for its fame. On both sides of the said strait lay Danish provinces Scania (Skåne) and Zealand (Sjælland). The island of Ven was quiet and peaceful. Hugues de Terlon noted in his *Mémoires* that there were two houses, a lot of rabbits and hares, so the Queen of Denmark liked to hunt there.[54] But the Northern War changed everything.

On the basis of the Roskilde peace treaty in 1658 the province of Scania was incorporated into Sweden, and the Öresund Strait became the border area separating two hostile kingdoms. The small island became significant in a military sense. During the enforcement of the provisions of the treaty in May 1658 a bitter dispute erupted: "over the island of Ven, which the Danes believed to be a part of Zealand, mainly for the reason that in no other province of Denmark peasants were serfs, and only in the places belonging to the island of Zealand. It was for this reason that the island of Ven was granted to Zealand some time before on the order of the court."[55] The Danes used all possible arguments and turned to a variety of documents: they cited the *History* of Arild Huitfeld, fiscal accounts of Ven, and recalled the judicial traditions and customs of the place. But the Swedes were not indolent, they presented a whole bunch of files and old stories. The parties were looking far into the past: "the history itself witnessed that the old border between the countries of Goths

---

[54] *Memoires de Chevalier de Terlon. Pour rendre compte au Roy, de ses Négociations, depuis l'année 1656 jusqu'en 1661. Tome premier. Suivant la Copie Imprimé à Paris Chez Louis Billaine* (Paris: Barbin, 1682), 106, 116.

[55] Pufendorf, *De Rebus*, 5: § 33, trans. W.K.

and Denmark was the strait of Öresund, or in the words of Pontanus Isaksen, Danish historian, in Öresund itself."[56] Terlon recorded that the Danish bishop of Scania played an inglorious role in the dispute as he supposedly equipped Swedes with a document confirming the connection of the island with the province of Scania[57].

According to Pufendorf, the Danes feared mostly that the Swedes would build a kind of fortress on the island, and hence assured that if Ven remained in their hands, they would never fortify it. However, in the end Charles Gustaw, "who was weary of this delay, since Ven was once a part of Scania, sent troops to the island as if to his property, as a result of which peasants swore an oath of allegiance to the Swedish king. Additionally, it appeared to be urgent to protect the port of Landskrona, which lay in front of the said island."[58]

The war on memory

The Northern War caused massive destruction, some of its traces are still visible. Only in the province of Małopolska in Southern Poland the number of households decreased by 38%.[59] The invaders, however, were not content with merely destroying and burning. According to the Swedish custom, established during the Thirty Years' War, they transported cultural assets such as libraries, sculptures, paintings as well as archives to their homeland. These robberies meant a great loss to the cultural heritage of Poland-Lithuania, and with reference to the archives it implied the possible impairment of the collective historical memory of the nation.

---

[56]   Pufendorf, *De Rebus*, 5: § 34, trans. W.K.
[57]   *Memoires de Chevalier de Terlon*, 116.
[58]   Pufendorf, *De Rebus*, 5: § 34, trans. W.K.
[59]   Józef A. Gierowski, *The Polish-Lithuanian Commonwealth in the XVIIIth Century. From anarchy to well organized state* (Kraków: Polska Akademia Umiejętności, 1996), 53; Józef A. Gierowski, *Rzeczpospolita w dobie złotej wolności (1648–1763)* (Kraków: Oficyna Wydawnicza "Fogra," 2001), 76.

Looting of the cultural property by the Swedes has been described in numerous works, first of all, an extensive book of Otto Walde constitutes a peculiar literary booty of the Swedes in their *age of power*.[60] Recently the subject has also been addressed by Dariusz Matelski, who described not only the process of looting, but also the efforts the Polish state invested concerning the restoration of the stolen documents.[61]

One of the biggest losses, noticeable in the Polish historiography to this very day, was a deportation of the Polish Crown Chancery Archive to Sweden, known also under the name of *Metrica Regni*. The term *Metrica* meant great archival fond, which was composed of the chancery record books, original parchment charters, different acts and inventories.[62] Happily enough, the Lithuanian Metrica, equivalent to the Crown Metrica, remained in the territory of the Grand Duchy of Lithuania during the war, and did not suffer much damage.

Yet, the value of the Crown Archives was considerably greater for the reason that it did not only serve the needs of the state authorities. Since the mid-sixteenth century the Crown Chancery Books were open to the public, which could be resultant upon relatively weak network of public notaries in Poland-Lithuania. The Crown Chancery filled the gap and began to record private documents. The extracts from the Chancery Books had a status of legal documents, or more specifically, they constituted testimonies of particular cases.[63] Such a legal state of affairs was confirmed by the highest authorities.

---

[60] Otto Walde, *Storhetstidens litterära krigsbyten*, vol. 1–2, (Stockholm: Almqvist och Wiksells Boktryk, 1916–20).

[61] Dariusz Matelski, "Straty polskich dóbr kultury w wojnach ze Szwecją w XVII i XVIII wieku oraz próby ich restytucji," *Archeion*, vol. 56 (2003): 118–138.

[62] Irena Sułkowska-Kurasiowa and Maria Woźniakowa, *Inwentarz Metryki Koronnej. Księgi wpisów i dekretów polskiej kancelarii królewskiej z lat 1447–1795* (Warszawa: Państwowe Wydawnictwo Naukowe, 1975), 7–12; Patricia Kennedy Grimsted, *The "Lithuanian Metrica" in Moscow and Warsaw. Reconstructing the Archives of the Grand Duchy of Lithuania* (Cambridge, MA: Published for the Harvard Ukrainian Research Institute, Harvard University, by Oriental Research Partners 1984), 4–10; Wojciech Krawczuk, *Metryka Koronna za Zygmunta III Wazy* (Kraków: Uniwersytet Jagielloński, 1995), 5–24.

[63] Wojciech Krawczuk, *Metrykanci koronni. Rozwój registratury centralnej od XVI do XVIII wieku* (Kraków: Historia Iagellonica, 2002), 19–23, 100, 115.

In 1585 at the Diet of the Commonwealth the King gave a statement, presented by Lord Marshall, that the "Metrica is open to everyone."[64] It was an unusual situation, since in early modern Europe the archives of the rulers were usually closed to the public. Thus the removal of these sources did not only mean problems for the administration of the Kingdom, but also real difficulties for individual persons.

Admittedly, Pufendorf informs about the scale of the destruction and looting. He quotes critical statements of diplomats, e.g. a warning by the French diplomat Antoine des Lumbres issued in autumn 1656: "The Poles were very bitter about the destruction of castles in various parts of their country, as well as about the rumour that Charles Gustav ordered the destruction of the Warsaw Royal Palaces and gardens, and also the pillaging and burning of the town – [de Lumbres] gently advised that this should not be done."[65]

We do not know whether Pufendorf's negative description of the Swedish actions in this respect resulted from his speedy work, which did not allow for "polishing" of the sources, or maybe it was again deliberate criticism? When the preliminary peace talks with Poland-Lithuania began in 1658, the Swedish commissioners received very clear instructions in regard to the looted Polish Crown Archives:

> If the Poles demanded the return of the documents from the Warsaw [Crown] Archives, the envoys should say that they could not accede to it, justifying [the Swedish side] that the Archives had already been taken away by the Poles themselves, before the Swedes came to Warsaw, or that it was dispersed later by the soldiers, and it could not be found.[66]

At that time, the Polish Crown Archives were already stored in Sweden and Swedish dignitaries were perfectly aware of this. In the Treaty of Oliva signed in 1660 the Swedes promised expressly that they would return it to Poland. The issue of the restitution of all the looted documents and archives, not only the Crown Archives, was

---

[64]   "Dyaryusze sejmowe r 1585," ed. Aleksander Czuczyński, Scriptores Rerum Polonicarum, vol. 18 (Kraków: Akademia Umiejętności, 1901) 51.
[65]   Pufendorf, De Rebus, 3: § 5, trans. W.K.
[66]   Pufendorf, De Rebus, 5: § 84, trans. W.K.

noted twice in the Treaty: in the eighth and ninth chapters.[67] The whole text of the Treaty was also printed as the annex of *De rebus*. As a result of these provisions, in the decades after 1660 the Kingdom of Poland regained much of the archival materials, mostly register books and privileges of the Polish Crown Metrica. These documents were arranged and recorded in Warsaw between the years 1672–1674 by the Metricant (officialy appointed Keeper of the Crown Chancery Books) Stephen Casimir Hankiewicz. However, he could not restore the original structure and fill the gaps in this fond. To this day the Swedish archives, among others, Riksarkivet in Stockholm, possess huge collections of documents which were looted during the Second Northern War in Poland. These are especially letters and auxiliary materials of many chanceries, to a large degree the Polish Crown Chancery.[68] From time to time the archivists find there unknown sources.[69]

Unquestionably, retention of these materials in Sweden was a clear breach of the provisions of the Oliva Treaty. Even greater problem stemmed from restricted access to these materials. The situation changed for the better only in the recent decades. For several hundred years the Polish archives and libraries lay forgotten in Sweden as they were not attractive for scientists of this country and only now they are reclaimed and used more intensively by the Polish historians. Yet this is in not just the case of the Polish archives – the so-called *occupation-archive* of great Novgorod sank as well into such oblivion. Only recently it was carefully inventoried in Riksarkivet.[70]

---

[67]   The Oliva Treaty in electronic form is available on the website of Leibniz – Institut für Europäische Geschichte Mainz in the database IEG – Friedensverträge, available from http://www.ieg-mainz.de/friedensvertraege [4 June 2014].

[68]   "Medeltiden. Kungl. Maj:ts kansli. Utrikesförvaltningen," Del 1. Band 2, ed. James Cavaille and Jan Lindroth, in *Riksarkivet beståndsöversikt* (Stockholm, 1996), 651–653.

[69]   Polish side organized many archival expeditions to Sweden. The greatest results were obtained by the scientific mission completed in 1911 by the historians of Akademia Umiejętności (Academy of Arts and Sciences). Edward Barwiński, Ludwik Birkenmajer and Jan Łoś, *Sprawozdanie z poszukiwań w Szwecji dokonanych z ramienia Akademii Umiejętności* (Kraków: Akademia Umiejętności, 1914).

[70]   Elisabeth Löfstrand and Laila Nordquist, *Accounts of an Occupied City. Catalogue of the Novgorod Occupation Archives, 1611–1617*, Series 1. Skrifter utgivna av Riksarkivet 24 (Stockholm, 2005).

Terlon noted that during the Danish War in 1658 the King of Sweden took the library from the castle of Ringsted worth fifty thousand ducats.[71] Such robberies were not infrequent.

The *war on memory* also denoted that attempts were made to destroy other manifestations and symbols recognized as hostile. That is why the famous Sigismund's Column in Warsaw was planned to be removed during the Swedish occupation of the town – as it showed King Sigismund, founder of the Polish Vasa dynasty, archenemy of the Swedish branch of Vasa dynasty. Charles Gustav wanted to diminish the importance of the Column in the centre of Warsaw, since it constituted a salient point of the monumental *Forum Vasorum*.[72] These actions, however, were not limited only to Poland-Lithuania. Pufendorf notes that during the peace talks with the Danes in 1660, the Swedish side put forward i.a. such demands:

> The images that were done to ridicule the Swedes were to be covered with other colours. The so-called "Jus Feciale" and "Manifestum Danicum," were to be ignored in the future, their print was to be prohibited. The mocking letters, written and published in Denmark also had to be destroyed. These were: "Speculum fidei Daniae, perfidiaeque Svecicae" and "Dissertatio Politico – Historica de detentione Legati Svecici Hafniae" and others by Gunde Rosencrantz. Finally, their creators were forbidden to participate in the conventions, where the affairs of the kingdoms [of Sweden and Denmark] were to be discussed, and additionally, they were not allowed to sign or seal the following Treaty.[73]

Conclusions

Pufendorf was well versed in the games of diplomats and actions of different chanceries. Of course some events he described were investigated many times after *De rebus...* was published and are not a revelation. But on the other hand, his comments on the minor issues and practices reveal a way of thinking and acting of early modern

---

[71] *Memoires de Chevalier de Terlon*, 106.

[72] Juliusz Chróścicki, *Sztuka i polityka. Funkcje propagandowe sztuki za Wazów 1587–1668* (Warszawa: Państwowe Wydawnictwo Naukowe, 1983), 230–231.

[73] Pufendorf, *De Rebus*, 7: § 26, trans. W.K.

clerks and diplomatic agents. Undeniably, there were substantial dif-
ferences in the approach to handling the matters in early modern
Europe – from the pragmatic to the complex and ceremonial. We
can also learn a lot about the functioning of the offices, about their
structures and power. There are also explicit signs of the existence of
double diplomacy: official and unofficial. The investigation of their
coexistence and cooperation/competition could add a lot to our
understanding of the problem. The question of the organization of
foreign policy in the epoch of the Second Northern War is as well
suspended and unexplained in many significant areas. But just then,
in the mid-seventeenth century, the diplomatic practice was created,
which is often in force even now.

Some of the tools used by the secretaries are applicable to the
present day, but many others, such as the exploitation of heraldry in
diplomacy are known only to a small group of historians and enthu-
siasts. Currently, the auxiliary sciences of history are in a deepening
crisis, mainly due to the significant limitation on lecturing at the
universities, which is even more regrettable since they could be of
great use in analyzing the early modern language of power, full of
half-forgotten symbols and signs. Pufendorf offers in this regard a
considerable support. The court ceremonies – precisely orchestrat-
ed, ways of welcoming and addressing the officials – are presented
lavishly and give an idea of the life at the Baroque court. The flow of
information, problems related to the creation of permanent postal
links, organization of congresses and diplomatic conventions, and
finally, early modern propaganda, are presented with great care in
the *Seven Books*.

Huge cultural losses that were caused in the Northern War are felt
to this very day, especially in the area of the archival science and dip-
lomatics. The destruction or removal of important historical sources
had a particularly large impact on the research possibilities of the
early modern central administration of Poland-Lithuania, especially
the state chanceries. Despite the provisions of the Treaty of Oliva in
1660, such damages were not fully repaired, although the possibilities existed. Every new track found, every comment of the contem-

poraries is important in this context. Fortunately, a change in the perception of the role of archives and the introduction of the concept of the joint heritage improved the situation allowing free access to the collections.[74]

---

[74] See the remarks on the concept of joint heritage by Eric Katelaar, "Documents as monuments," *Archeion*, vol. 62 (2011): 57.

Chapter V: War on the water

The Count Palatine Sulzbach tried to win the island of Møn, which was defended by hundred Danish cavalrymen and five hundred armed peasants. At the very beginning he was repelled. Because of the shallow sea he could not get close to the shore and had to temporarily abandon his plan. [...] Then, in the town of Nykøbing, on the Falster island, the Swedes prepared flat-bottomed ferries. Each one of them could take fifty horses on the lower deck; the upper part, in turn, was made of thick planks in the shape of a shaft, which was to serve the infantry. The cavalry could easily go ashore. The fire of the infantry muskets from the upper deck prevented the access of the enemies to the coast. Initially, the ferries were directed towards the place where they usually moored, therefore, everyone who was on the island could reach the place to ward off the landing of the Swedes. But then the Swedes rowed to another place. The soldiers landed ashore so quickly that those few Danes who defended the coast could not repulse the attack. The Swedes lined up in ranks, and after a fierce battle forced the attacking Danes to flee, of whom seventy were killed. In this way the Swedes invaded the island of Møn.[1]

The military efforts of the Second Northern War were conducted on land and at sea with equal fervour. The two largest maritime power at that time: the English State's Navy (since the execution of Charles I, not Royal any more) and the Dutch Navy, took part in the blockades and encounters.[2] The great naval battle fought in Öresund on 29th October 1658, between the Dutch and the Swedish fleet, passed into a legend since the "Dutch themselves admitted that they had never been in such a fierce fight."[3] However, apart from great naval engage-

---

[1] Samuel Pufendorf, *De rebus a Carolo Gustavo Sveciae Rege, gestis commentariorum libri septem, elegantissimis tabulis aeneis exornati cum triplici indice* (Nuremberg 1696), 6: § 8, trans. W.K.

[2] Jan Glete, *Swedish Naval Administration, 1521–1721. Resource Flows and Organisational Capabilities* (Leiden: Brill, 2010), 105–112, 175–184; Nicholas Andrew Martin Rodger, *The Command of the Ocean. A Naval History of Britain 1649–1815* (London: Penguin Books in association with the National Maritime Museum, 2004), 29.

[3] Pufendorf, *De rebus*, 5: § 104, trans. W.K.

ments, which are already thoroughly examined, many other issues, related to the water hazards and obstacles, often constitute decisive elements of the campaigns of the Second Northern War. The most famous event in the category of "Other Actions" was the crossing of the entire Swedish army over the ice of the Little and Great Belt Straits. The Swedes headed successfully for Danish islands in winter 1658. The success of this most daring expedition broke down the opponents. The land army turned for a short time into the army of the sea.[4] Until now, the Swedish historians have been extensively discussing the details of this action, and in particular, who conducted reconnaissance and who examined the thickness of ice.

These were, undeniably, extraordinary achievements. On a daily basis, though, all the armies involved carried out many different actions related to the water. Especially risky were river or strait crossings. From today's point of view such undertakings are important, yet not decisive, as the engineer units are now superbly equipped. In the seventeenth century, however, the ability to conduct the crossing was an essential indicator of the skills of the officers and soldiers. Hence Pufendorf paid particular attention to such ventures. In April 1657 the Swedes were embittered: "as the people of Prince Rákóczy did not demonstrate appropriate diligence [in the construction of the bridge], or lacked experience in such operations, moreover, they had to use the Swedish bridge. Because of this delay, the King lost a perfect opportunity to destroy the surprised enemy."[5]

The importance and difficulty of the crossings were so high that the courtiers of Louis XIV chose the "Crossing of the Rhine" by French forces in 1672 as a feat equal to those of the ancient heroes, as a result of which the King was praised and portrayed by the most eminent poets and artists.[6] In the Eastern European theatre of war

---

[4]   Summary of the previous studies, see: Lars Ericsson Wolke, *1658 Tåget över Bält* (Lund: Historiska Media, 2008); Robert I. Frost, *Northern Wars. War, State and Society in Northeastern Europe, 1558–1721* (Harlow: Longman, 2000), 180.

[5]   Pufendorf, *De rebus*, 4: § 14, trans. W.K.

[6]   Peter Burke, *The Fabrication of Louis XIV* (New Haven–London: Yale University Press, 1994), 84–91. The action was presented in such a way as if the whole French army crossed the Rhine, and factually only two cavalry regiments performed the feat. John Childs, *War-*

such achievements seem much more frequent. Anyway the echo of some actions on the water lives to this very day. In the Polish national anthem from 1797 we are called to follow Stefan Czarniecki, who after the Swedish occupation returned home across the sea to save the country – which is a vague reference to Czarniecki's struggles in Denmark, probably to his landing on the island of Als in 1658.[7]

At times the combined actions on land and sea were quite remarkable due to the formations used. So it was in October 1657 when the Swedish army carried out a huge assault on the powerful Danish coastal fortress Frederiksodde. The infantry carried out the attack from the land, the cavalry from the sea.

> Wrangel decided to strike two bastions located closest to the sea, on the side of the Middelfart Strait, using four brigades under the colonels: Nils Brahe, Per Larsson Sparre, Fabian Fersen and Spens. Johan Georg, Prince of Anhalt, with two regiments of horse was to break into the town by a circuitous route through the shallow water near the bastion. […] Prince of Anhalt and his cavalry crossed the water next to the two rows of palisades, but when they reached the third row, the water proved to be too deep to be waded. Therefore, some of the riders dismounted and cut the piles down with axes, making the way for troops who later invaded the town. They met a rank of foot soldiers and attacked them just as soon as they fired a volley of muskets. [The Danish soldiers] were assaulted violently and dispersed. At that time the [Swedish] infantry entered the shaft and attacked the enemy so savagely that although [the Danes] made a brave defence, they had to yield one position after another.[8]

At times we may encounter other descriptions resembling action films of our time, where small units of selected elite soldiers inflict heavy losses on the enemy:

> In September 1656 the Swedes, besieged in Riga, made preparations for a raid across the river. They put two hundred foot soldiers into the boats, which, under the command of Captain Zeddelmann, floated in the dark night against the current half a mile up the river, and landed near the Russian camp on the so-called

---

fare in the Seventeenth Century, Smithsonian History of Warfare (Washington: Smithsonian Books, 2004), 167.

[7] Adam Kersten, *Stefan Czarniecki* (Warszawa: Wydawnictwo Ministerstwa Obrony Narodowej, 1963), 387–391. In the lyrics of "Hakkapeliittain Marssi" as well (the March of the Finnish Cavalry), written as late as in 1872 by Zacharias Topelius, we read that the Finnish cavalrymen "swam across the Vistula as happy as if they were to attend a feast."

[8] Pufendorf, *De rebus*, 4: § 75, trans. W.K.

Dietrichs-Werder island, where the Russians stored large amount of war materials. When [the Swedes] went ashore, they pretended to be Muscovites and killed the guards on the island. They set fire to three boats filled with gunpowder, war materials and food, and the buildings that were constructed for the production of incendiary bombs. Hence loud bang and flames that ignited suddenly led to great confusion in the camp of the Russians, as a result of which their whole army stood guard during the night.[9]

As Jeremy Black has reminded recently, the small-scale fights on the coasts and rivers have usually not been accentuated in the works of military historians. Such a lack of interest affects not only the military history of distant continents but also this of Northern and Eastern Europe.[10] It seems, however, that Pufendorf fled successfully from such allegations and acknowledged the actions on the water as legitimate grounds for the military glory, giving us also an opportunity to study such events.

Water as weapon

Fortifications of the town of Gdańsk were the most powerful in the Polish-Lithuanian Commonwealth. The necessity for their construction originated mainly from the time of the attack on Prussia by the army of Gustavus Adolphus in the years 1626–1629. As a consequence, the process of modernization of this defence system accelerated not only in the cities of Royal Prussia. New fortifications had to protect watercourses as well. This was of paramount importance, since the downstream Vistula River is divided into several branches before it flows into the Gdańsk Bay.[11] Two most important branches are *Leniwka* – on the left and *Nogat* – on the right, between which lies delta of the Vistula River, the big river island of very fertile soil, called Żuławy Malborskie (*Marienburger Werder*).

---

[9]   Pufendorf, *De rebus*, 3: § 52, trans. W.K.
[10] Jeremy Black, *Rethinking Military History* (New York: Routledge, 2008), 22–23.
[11] Jerzy Stankiewicz, "System fortyfikacyjny Gdańska i okolicy w czasie wojny 1655–1660 r.," *Studia i Materiały do Historii Wojskowości*, vol. 20 (1976): 74–121.

From the very beginning of the Northern War in 1655, the town of Gdańsk was loyal to the Polish King, John Casimir. This fidelity was one of the key factors determining the final defeat of the Swedes. The Dutchmen, in turn, acted as powerful guardians of the town, very anxious to maintain high degree of town's autonomy and support the defence of Gdańsk by virtue of diplomatic and maritime actions.[12]

The Swedes were focused on attacking the outer fortifications of the town, in which they achieved some success: notably in 1656, when they managed to win the important fort called Gdańska Głowa (*Danziger Haupt*), located in the other bifurcation of the Vistula between *Leniwka* and *Szkarpawa* branches.[13] Gdańsk alone, hidden behind its massive bastions, remained beyond the reach of any assault, even the naval blockade proved to be ineffective. Already in 1656 the Swedes decided to use a special attack tool, namely the water. Charles Gustav ordered Gustav Otto Stenbock "to destroy the floodgates on the Radunia River near Pruszcz (*Praust*) which kept the river in its bed. The water turned elsewhere, which caused that numerous mills of Gdańsk became useless."[14] Even worse was to come. The protracted land and sea blockade of the town forced the Swedes to look for rather unusual solutions.

> To chastise the insolence [of Gdańsk], the King decided to direct the water of the Vistula to its right branch so that the other arm of the river which flows near Gdańsk would be unfit for sailing ships. It was also believed that the water would fall into the sea slower so that the estuary would be filled with sand. The King, however, wanted first to check if the threat itself would not change the bad attitude of the burghers. Therefore, he announced his intentions to the Dutch envoys – to warn the burghers of Gdańsk to limit their plans and prevent such calamity. [The burghers] heard the news not without fear, knowing well enough that the town would fall if the port was closed. Yet they ignored the intentions of the King, for they did not believe that they were true, or they doubted the possibility of executing the said plan.[15]

---

[12] Edmund Cieślak, "Okres 'potopu' szwedzkiego," in *Historia Gdańska*, vol. 3, ed. Edmund Cieślak (Gdańsk: Instytut Historii PAN, Zakład Historii Gdańska i Dziejów Morskich Polski, 1993), 36–56.

[13] Stankiewicz, "System," 89.

[14] Pufendorf, *De rebus*, 3: § 17; Jerzy Stankiewicz, "Przemiany przestrzenne i demograficzne Gdańska," in *Historia Gdańska*, vol. 3, 22.

[15] Pufendorf, *De rebus*, 4: § 17, trans. W.K.

Nonetheless, the burghers of Gdańsk were wrong, and the King of Sweden was determined to destroy their trade. The Swedes prepared a detailed plan to bar the left arm of the Vistula River, i.e. Leniwka, the water was to enter the right branch – Szkarpawa.[16]

> The curved dam was built near the Montauer Spitze, where the Vistula is divided into two branches,[17] but also at the Danziger Haupt on the left arm. [The Swedes] sank many boats filled with rocks, consequently the water had to flow only into the right branch of the Vistula River. The dam was just high enough for the ice floe to pass over. Then, when the spring waters of the Vistula increased, the Swedes broke off the dikes, twelve cubits wide, near the village of Kiezmark, and the great mass of water flooded the most fertile fields of Żuławy Gdańskie (Danziger Werder) destroying the buildings around.[18] When the burghers of Gdańsk conducted a raid and managed to repair the damage, the Swedes broke dikes somewhere else, closer to their ramparts. The Swedes prevented their reconstruction firing cannons from nearby fortifications. Undeniably, the said actions caused serious harm to the fields of Gdańsk, yet damage, on the whole, was not as severe as it had been hoped, since the tremendous momentum of the ice floes lifted part of the obstacles. Therefore, the arm of the river near Gdańsk was still navigable and it flew into the sea. Neither was it confirmed that the sand closed the mouth of the river.[19]

The crossings of Lech and San Rivers

Forcing the San River in April 1656 is one of the most brilliant manoeuvres in the long list of Charles Gustav's victories. It was identified by the Swedes as one of the four most important battles of the Second Northern War. To commemorate it, an inscription was carved on the equestrian monument of the King in Stockholm in front of the Nordiska Museet.[20] The King with his army managed to escape from a desperate plight, when driven into a small area where the San River

---

[16] Stankiewicz, "System," 93.

[17] The Monatuer Spitze lies at another fork of the Vistula River, where the current is divided into Leniwka and Nogat branches.

[18] In this case there are some doubts, as some historians believe that the burghers themselves flooded the fields to hinder the enemy access to the town walls. Cieślak, "Okres 'potopu' szwedzkiego," 41.

[19] Pufendorf, De rebus, 4: § 17, trans. W.K.

[20] The monument was erected in 1917. Björn Asker, Karl X Gustav: en biografi (Lund: Historiska Media, 2009, 2nd edition 2010), 14.

flows into the Vistula. He was surrounded by a much larger Polish-Lithuanian force. Charles Gustav surprised opponents, made a bold stroke across the San under heavy fire of the Lithuanians, crushed them, and escaped from the snare.[21]

The known descriptions of this crossing remind us of similar actions of Gustav Adolf, master of reconnaissance and daring plans. If we were to look for a Swedish "speciality" in early modern warfare, such engagements can actually provide us with some clues. In the May of 1631 Gustav Adolf forced the Lech River and secured a major victory over the experienced imperial commander Johan Tilly. Michael Roberts points to the extensive experience of the Swedish troops in such operations, as they were conducted earlier in the war.[22] During the Lech crossing there were several separate phases. First, the Swedes tried to confuse the enemy, they pretended to attack in some other places, and while they were setting fire to dry grass, they sought to hide the area of the real crossing. They prepared a floating bridge, established bridge-head on the other side of the river and supported it with strong reinforcements. The Swedish cavalry forded the Lech River elsewhere and attacked the enemy flanks in parallel. Tilly felt too safe, assuming that the river itself gave him a sufficient protection, the Lithuanians under the command of Paweł Sapieha in 1656 made the same mistake.

Accordingly, Charles Gustav decided to use one beneficial feature of the site. He ordered his carpenters to build a bridge in front of the islet that was in the middle of the San River. It was an unenviable task, for the Lithuanians built the ramparts on the opposite shore along the river and harassed the working party with heavy fire from cannons and muskets. Almost all the Swedish carpenters were killed, and consequently the bridge could not be finished. It covered only one arm of the San, up to the islet in the current, and the other arm was a bit wider.[23]

---

[21] Frost, *Northern Wars*, 173.

[22] Michael Roberts, *Gustavus Adolphus. A History of Sweden 1611–1632*, vol. 2 (Edinburgh: Longmans, Green & Co., 1957), 700.

[23] Pufendorf, *De rebus*, 3: § 12; Paweł Skworoda, *Warka–Gniezno 1656* (Warszawa: Dom Wydawniczy "Bellona," 2003), 127–128.

Because it was not safe to remain in this place any longer, so as not to give the Poles, who were positioned on the other side of the Vistula, enough time to join the Lithuanians, the King made a bold decision to cross the River San in front of the enemy and take position on the opposite side to avoid ultimate danger at all costs. Charles Gustav ordered to set fifty cannons on the river bank, place the infantry in the ranks, with the cavalry behind, to the amazement of the enemy watching from the opposite riverbank, since they could not guess what the King intended. To deceive them and to cause confusion, the King ordered colonels Gustav Kruus and Dietrich de la Chapelle to board three boats with three hundred infantry and to lead them in secret to the small island in the middle of the San River. Once they heard the thunder of cannons and the noise of drums and trumpets, they had to cross over the river, take up position and defend it fiercely. Since there were no more boats, they had to promptly send these three back so that more troops could cross.

This bold venture was successful. When the dusk was falling, the Swedish cannons opened fire at the Lithuanian camp. The noise of trumpets and the roar of drums reverberated everywhere. Soon the King commanded the infantry to pass the bridge to reach the islet and get to the part of the bridge which was still under construction. At that time, Kruus and la Chapelle crossed the second arm of the river by boats, and under cover of bushes they took the nearby Lithuanian ramparts and occupied their positions. The enemies took up arms in a daze, not knowing where to turn, as they had already seen the Swedes in their camp, and knew well that the bridge was not completed. However, at least initially, they fired many cannons and muskets from their entrenchments, causing considerable damage to the Swedish infantry. One cannonball flew between King's legs, yet did not inflict any damage, just threw dust into his face and clothing. But then, when the Lithuanians saw the Swedes in their ramparts, they were so terrified that the King with his whole army dared to threaten them from the rear that they ran out of the camp with horror, leaving the cannons, banners and all the baggage trains. [...] Next day the whole (Swedish) army crossed the river, fleeing the greatest danger so far.[24]

The booty was abundant. Pufendorf notes that in the Lithuanian camp the Swedes found eighteen bronze cannons, and some iron ones, twenty-eight streamers, hundreds of wagons, lots of animals and food and feed, which supported the starving army considerably, as well as many prisoners. Ironically, such a great Swedish victory received insignificant coverage at the European courts. The Poles and Lithuanians were so convinced that they would be victorious that they spread the news of their great triumph even before a decisive clash. It seems that in the propaganda warfare they had greater successes (and perhaps experience) than the Swedes. In Eastern and

---

[24] Pufendorf, *De rebus*, 3: § 12, trans. W.K.

Northern Europe, where the network of roads and infrastructure was poorly developed, such engineering skills were as vital for the survival of an army as the well-prepared plans.[25]

Pirates and diplomats

The issue of the organization of the war at sea by the Polish-Lithuanian Commonwealth has been thoroughly examined in the Polish historiography.[26] One might even say that the said topic has been accentuated too strongly for the reasons of prestige and politics of the Polish state in the twentieth century. The efforts of the Polish kings in this regard were described excessively and much emphasis was laid on the naval warfare, although in reality the Polish-Lithuanian actions on the sea were greatly limited, while the successes rare. Such attitude of the Polish historians, both in the interwar period and after World War II, stemmed from a fully understandable patriotic fervour and hope for a closer linkage between the Polish state and society and the Baltic Sea. To this day the readers are eager to learn more about the adventures of the *guardians of the sea* – privateers, who served Sigismund II Augustus, the King of Poland, and were especially active at sea during the First Northern War in the years 1563–1570.[27]

Recently Bohdan A. Kuliński has returned to this theme while analyzing the old sources. He convincingly depicted both the issue and historiographical considerations by describing the history and legend of the famous galleon from Elbląg, built by Venetian masters

---

[25] Erik A. Lund, "The Scientific Revolution and Generalship in the Habsburg Army, 1686–1723," in *Warfare in Eastern Europe, 1500–1800*, ed. Brian L. Davies (Leiden–Boston: Brill, 2012), 228–240.

[26] This section is based mainly on my paper delivered at the Baltic Colloquium (*Polonica w zbiorach państw nadbałtyckich*) held on 30th November 2012 in the Central Archives of Historical Records (Archiwum Główne Akt Dawnych) in Warsaw.

[27] The most frequently used Polish term for a privateer is *kaper*. Andrzej Groth, "Czasy Rzeczypospolitej szlacheckiej," in *Historia Pucka* (Gdańsk: Wydawnictwo "Marpress," 1998), 97–101.

in the years 1570–1572, which in the end turned out to be a galley, not a galleon[28]. Also the period of the Swedish Deluge was examined by other historians in the aspect of fighting at sea, analogously to the actions of the privateers. The most important in this respect was the policy of the town of Gdańsk, which throughout the war had both the means and abilities to carry out such ventures. Charles Gustav was well aware of the importance of the town, and therefore, at the very beginning of the war, the Swedes tried to set naval blockade of Gdańsk and establish customs duty at sea, which, in turn, outraged both the Dutch and Oliver Cromwell.

When it comes to the privateers from Gdańsk, their most audacious adventure was probably the seizure of the Swedish ship with the famous General Hans Christoffer Königsmarck on board. This happened in 1656 in the roadsted of the town.

> For the Swedes the capture of Königsmarck was not an insignificant event. At the request of the King he sailed from Wismar to Prussia with a company of Scots contracted by Cranstone. When they passed the shore of Gdańsk, the Scots rebelled and forced the captain of the ship to land on the coast, where the enemy ships arrived and took Königsmarck as a prisoner to the town. They carried him into the fortress of Wisłoujście (Weichselmünde), where he stayed until the end of the war. Charles Gustav used the mediation of Dutch envoys and turned to the burghers of Gdańsk asking for Königsmarck's release. He indicated that he did not run out of means to punish their pride and could protect his navigation against their robbery. He trusted in the renewed alliance with the Dutch, in which the town of Gdańsk was also included, and the burghers did not protest against having been subjected to this treaty.[29]

Charles Gustav repeatedly attempted to release General Königsmarck in exchange for some distinguished Poles held as captives by the Swedes, but with no success.

We also know of yet another action of the privateers from Gdańsk which happened in 1656. "At the end of this year, the Danes showed evidence of their attitude towards the Swedes. They informed the burghers of Gdańsk of the arrival of a Dutch ship carrying gunpowder

---

[28]   Bohdan Andrzej Kuliński, *Okręt Jego Królewskiej Mości Zygmunta Augusta. Historia galeonu, który nie był galeonem* (Warszawa: Warszawska Firma Wydawnicza, 2012), 7–8, 105–174, 233–239.

[29]   Pufendorf, *De rebus*, 3: § 38, trans. W.K.

to Pillau. The burghers immediately sent light privateer ships from their port. They seized the sailor, took the powder but sent the ship with the rest of the transported goods to Pillau."[30] Knowing the dislike of the Dutch for Charles Gustav, we may suspect that they themselves informed Gdańsk about the departure of this merchantman.

There are some specific terminological nuances in the sources: the party which used the services of the privateers gave them the name of *cursores maritimes*, or corsairs, and the affected side, in this case the Swedes, named them far stronger, as *pirates*. It seemed that there was no time for a deep legal analysis of documents. Was a privateer ship equipped with the appropriate commission? Or perhaps it was an ordinary robber, also a sea pirate? At the early stage of the war the success of the action itself was much more important. However, with time, some legal complications arose.

Let us now turn to the issues of such diplomatic problems. It would seem that Edmund Cieślak was right when recapitulating quite pessimistically the attempts of King John Casimir to create a privateer fleet: "it is not known what practical effects resulted from these efforts of the King, but presumably these were mostly irrelevant."[31] Such a privateer fleet could be established in Gdańsk only, yet the town was very reluctant to assist in the creation of any sea force, which would be independent of the town council. Gdańsk had enough of its own ships and the burghers were sure that in case of emergency the Dutch fleet would arrive carrying armed support. This expectation was confirmed during the war, when the Dutch warships stood in the roadstead of Gdańsk and the Dutch infantry took part in the defence of the town fortifications.

It seems, however, that the Polish privateer actions were undertaken, but further away from Gdańsk, and what is more, they left a significant mark on the diplomatic game, which was carried out after the conclusion of peace treaty between Sweden and Denmark in Roskilde on 26th February 1658. Soon after signing the peace, Charles

---

[30] Pufendorf, *De rebus*, 3: § 92, trans. W.K.
[31] Cieślak, "Okres 'potopu' szwedzkiego," 43.

Gustav was already frantically looking for an excuse to begin a new war with Denmark. The case of Polish privateers appeared in the background of another, much more important issue, the so-called "matters of Guinea," which will be discussed later in the text. These activities were presented among many reasons for the start of the second Danish War in August 1658.

In the spring of 1658, and thus before the start of the second Danish War, the Danes and the Swedes held noncommittal talks about the possibilities of an alliance. They also debated various dilemmas arising from the Treaty of Roskilde. Among other issues Pufendorf records the following case: "on 14th May 1658 a dispute sparked concerning the merchantman from Norrköping in Sweden, which was captured near the island of Rügen by the sea pirates, even before the declaration of war. The Danes refused to give it back saying that it was gained on the orders of Poles. It was clear, however, that the privateer was armed in Copenhagen, and even the booty was transported there. No doubt the reason for the refusal was the participation of more than one great lord of Denmark in the said plunder."[32]

During further negotiations, the Danes would not allow that any record was made in the arrangement referring to the abducted merchant ship from Norrköping. The Swedes had to settle for a Royal word that this matter would be brought to justice. However, the Swedes were not content and stated firmly: "Since the privateer excused himself that he was equipped with the Polish orders, the case is public. It had to be decided if the Polish King had any right to disturb the Baltic Sea by any means and the said issue should also enter the agreement as a good example. Charles Gustav indeed had to recognize such orders of the King of Poland as an action which affected the specific laws of both Kingdoms [i.e. of Sweden and Denmark]. He was very surprised that the Danes wanted to turn a blind eye to the fact that a Polish corsair dared to use the ports of Denmark, and that their citizens, who served the Poles in this way, did not suffer any serious penalties."[33]

---

[32] Pufendorf, *De rebus*, 5: § 35, trans. W.K.
[33] Pufendorf, *De rebus*, 5: § 40, trans. W.K.

Indeed, John Casimir issued such documents for privateers or corsairs. Władysław Czapliński published a Royal letter on the matter, dated at 16th July 1659, addressed to the town council of Gdańsk.[34] The King informed the burghers that he gave certain individuals marine passports (*Seepässe*), under which they could attack the enemy ships. The ships were to be equipped at the expense of those non-specified persons. As hostility of Gdańsk towards the idea of creating of an independent privateer fleet was already widely known, the letter was most probably submitted post factum. We do not know, however, whether these privateer ships' crews were composed of the citizens of the Polish-Lithuanian Commonwealth, or of the Danes, or what flags they flew to identify their affiliation. Perhaps a thorough research in the well preserved Danish archives could provide us with the answers. The Danish envoys arriving at John Casimir's court in the time of war had verbal instructions and they passed them during confidential audiences.[35] We know with certainty that the ships were equipped in the Danish ports, and most probably also some contracts regarding the distribution of spoils were concluded there. The King of Poland also cooperated closely with Frederick III Oldenburg, King of Denmark, in regard to the activities at sea.

Denmark could secure the aid of the great naval power of the Netherlands, but as it turned out, it did not despise the support of the Polish-Lithuanian Commonwealth. In some circumstances, even the use of the flag of the Commonwealth could be beneficial and helpful in distancing the claims of the Swedes. To show the momentum of the King Frederik III's actions, the most famous privateer expedition of the Northern War requires being recalled – unfortunately, this time without the participation of the Polish ships.

---

[34] Władysław Czapliński, "Projekt utworzenia floty kaperskiej w czasie 'potopu' szwedzkiego," *Rocznik Gdański*, vol. 13 (1954), 131–132.

[35] *Res Polonicae ex Archivo Regni Daniae*, ed. Carolina Lanckorońska et Georgius Steen Jensen, *Elementa ad fontium editiones*, vol. 20 (Roma: Institutum Historicum Polonicum Romae, 1969), 198–199, no. 203.

The African dimension

Therefore, let us go to the south, into the hot area of the Gulf of Guinea in West Africa, where in the year 1650 a Swedish colony was established, founded by Louis de Geer, entrepreneur from the Netherlands.[36] De Geer obtained an appropriate privilege from Queen Christina and created the African Company (Swedish: *Afrikanska Kompaniet*) dominated by the Dutch. A little earlier a similar Swedish colony was created in North America, also with the help of the Dutch. However, in September 1655 it was occupied by the force from New Amsterdam, under the command of Pieter Stuyvesant, Director–General of the New Netherland colony.[37]

The central point of the Swedish colony in Africa was the former Portuguese fort *Cabo Corso*, located in the area of today's Cape Coast. The director and member of the company was Henrik Karloff, native of Rostock, associated with the Dutch merchants. Soon afterwards Karloff came into conflict with other shareholders. The allegations related to the fact that, contrary to the statute of the company, he ran his own, private trade in the area. He was eventually repaid by Laurens de Geer, the son of Louis and it seemed that the conflict ended. In 1656 the new governor, Johan Philip von Krusenstierna, began to administer the colony. Karloff had to leave, moved with his family from Hamburg to Embden and came into contact with the King of Denmark.

It turned out that Karloff's resentment against the Swedes was deep. In the early December 1657, having obtained the necessary authorization to privateer, he sailed on the Danish ship "Glückstadt"

---

[36] Erik Wilhelm Dahlgren, "Louis de Geer," in *Svenskt Biografiskt Lexikon*, vol. X (Stockholm: Albert Bonniers Förlag, 1931), 457–476. See also: Victor G. Granlund, *En svensk koloni i Afrika: eller svenska afrikanska kompaniets historia* (Stockholm: Norstedt, 1879); György Novaky, *Handelskompanier och kompanihandel: Svenska Afrikakompaniet 1649–1663: en studie i feodal handel*, Studia Historica Upsaliensia 159 (Uppsala: Almquist & Wiksell, 1990).

[37] Alan Taylor, *American Colonies. The Settling of North America* (London: Penguin, 2001), 254–255.

armed with eighteen guns and forty-eight people[38] from the port of Embden and set sail towards Ghana. He landed on its banks near the place called *Gemorie*, where the Swedish Company established its house.

> There he learned about the situation of the most important Swedish fortification, called Capo Cosso and headed on until Capo Tres Punctas, where he dropped the anchor. The Dutch lent him four large boats and forty-six black slaves. The following night he went ashore near Fort de Mina with twenty-two sailors and marched towards the Swedish fort located about a mile and a half from there. He gathered a number of natives from the neighbourhood and the slaves of the Swedish company, and in the morning, in the fog, when the gate was opened, he attacked the fort. Karloff occupied this place easily, captured the governor Krusenstierna and took all the goods and the vessel which was anchored at the shore. Immediately afterwards he raised the Danish flag to the fortifications and in accordance with the custom of the Danes signalled a salvo of guns. Subsequently, he captured smaller forts: Johanisburg and Annemabo, along with a small habitat Alcana so that the damage suffered by the company was estimated at three hundred thousand thalers.[39]

It was assessed that Karloff's gain was 185 kg of gold and a large amount of ivory. He returned with the booty to Glückstadt in June 1658, i.e. about four months after the conclusion of the peace treaty in Roskilde on 26th February. The Swedes demanded at once the reimbursement of damages, imprisonment of Karloff and of course his surrender to Sweden, nonetheless, he managed to escape with the plunder.

Yet, it did not resolve the matter. The so-called " Guinean case" and the issue of the Polish piracy, alongside other similar not very important issues, provided Charles Gustav with a very convenient excuse to start the Second Danish War in the summer of 1658. After the Karloff's attack and Dutch rule, Cabo Corso was temporarily occupied by indigenous people of the land, which may serve as an interesting example of an early act of decolonization, but also of a wide impact of the Second Northern War.[40]

---

[38] From the description we can make that it was probably a fast and manoeuvrable brig, pirate's favourite.

[39] Pufendorf, *De rebus*, 5: § 39, trans. W.K.

[40] Pufendorf, *De rebus*, 6: § 59, trans. W.K.

Dominium Maris Baltici

We should pay attention to the arguments of the Swedes in the aforementioned dispute, since it clearly shows how the Swedish diplomats and King Charles Gustav understood the concept of the Baltic Sea Dominion in the mid-seventeenth century. Ordinarily, we assume that the term means the struggle for supremacy in the Baltic region, and that the Kingdoms of Sweden and Denmark were the main rivals in securing the coastal area around this water.[41] Well, the Swedes in those days did not think so. They believed that *Dominium Maris Baltici* is their obvious right, the legal custom, according to which only the kings of Sweden and Denmark could maintain armed fleets on the Baltic Sea. In their view other rulers, be it Tsar of Russia, King of Poland or Elector of Brandenburg, were not entitled to the possession of the navy at all. Therefore, the Swedes did not have to seek a *dominium maris*, because in their understanding they already had it. They had only to maintain it against other competitors.

The issue of the sea dominion appeared repeatedly during the Second Northern War, even in the Swedish talks in 1656 with Elector Frederick William of Brandenburg, at the time when Charles Gustav was very keen on the cooperation with the said Prince. But when the Elector expressed a wish to arm two or three warships to protect his ports, the King forbade his envoys to negotiate the topic. "The King ordered that if diplomatic agents of the Elector insisted on this issue, his representatives had to point out that as the Elector obtained full power [in the Duchy of Prussia], he also gained the rights of the Polish Crown, which had never had any claims to maintain the fleet on the Baltic Sea. And even when the Poles attempted to build their fleet, the Kings of the North [i.e. of Sweden and Denmark] hindered the implementation of such plans."[42] Already in 1654 a rumour circulated, arousing great indignation at the Swedish court, that King John Casimir was allegedly planning an alliance with the Netherlands or

---

[41] Frost, *Northern Wars*, 3–7, 21.
[42] Pufendorf, *De rebus*, 3: § 36, trans. W.K.

Denmark, under which a great fleet under the Polish flag would sail into the Baltic Sea.[43] However, there is every likelihood that it was one of many invented stories that were to pave the way for waging war against the Commonwealth.

To defend their dominion the Swedes were willing to defy even the most powerful navy in the world at that time – the Dutch fleet. "It consisted of thirty-five large and well-equipped warships and a similar one had not been seen in the Netherlands for eighty years. Behind them followed a great number of smaller vessels, carrying troops and provisions. Therefore, the Dutch could not imagine that the Swedish fleet would dare to start the fight. For if Sweden was defeated, the provinces of the King of Sweden would be open to the incursions of so many enemies. However, if the Dutch lost, they had enough assets to prepare a new fleet, and even if everything went wrong, the mediation of France and England always afforded an opportunity for reconciliation with Sweden on fair terms."[44] Despite these hopes, a bloody naval battle was fought in Öresund between the Dutch and the Swedish fleets on 29th October 1658. The Dutch managed to break the Swedish blockade of Copenhagen, but lost a large warship and thirteen smaller vessels, additionally, hundreds of people were killed and injured. Vice-admiral Witte Corneliszoon de With died of wounds after losing his ship "Brederode."[45] The losses of the Swedish fleet were even greater.[46] "The battle of Öresund cooled the impudence (of the Dutch), as they had never believed that the Swedes would be so brave and dare to fight against them. Indeed, the orders given to Admiral Obdam were strict: find and destroy the Swedish fleet without hesitation."[47]

---

[43] Pufendorf, *De rebus*, 1: § 43, trans. W.K.
[44] Pufendorf, *De rebus*, 5: § 103, trans. W.K.
[45] Lena Ånimmer, "Ett krigsbyte från 1658," in *När sundet blev gräns. Till mine av Roskildefreden*, "Årsbok för Riksarkivet och landsarkiven 2008" (Växjö 2008), 45–50.
[46] Claes-Göran Isacson, *Karl X Gustavs krig. Fälttågen i Polen, Tyskland, Baltikum, Danmark och Sverige 1655–1660* (Lund: Historiska Media, 2004), 208–215.
[47] Pufendorf, *De rebus*, 5: § 110, trans. W.K.

Conclusions

The ability to deal with water hazards seems to be a significant indicator of professionalism of any early modern army. In particular, the issues of crossings and attacks of land forces by water perfectly show the state of the forces involved.

King John Casimir Vasa appears once again as an underestimated ruler. It transpires that he took advantage of every opportunity and even in the deepest crisis he was able to skilfully interact with the King of Denmark, contributing to a certain degree towards maritime activities. Moreover, he created a new legal situation in which one of the existing guards of *Dominium Maris Baltici* permitted the ships under the authority of the Polish-Lithuanian Commonwealth to fight on the Baltic Sea. Most often *The Swedish Deluge*, despite its aquatic references, is shown as the war waged primarily on the land, with its maritime activities neglected. The cooperation of the United Provinces of the Netherlands with the Kingdom of Denmark and with the Polish-Lithuanian Commonwealth in the time of the Second Northern War, and in particular the issue of the Dutch fleet operations on the Baltic Sea, exerted a tremendous impact on the development of that great struggle. Hopefully, in the recent years the subject has been further investigated, as evidenced by new publications.[48] The earlier negligence does not limit itself to the Polish historiography, as unconventional warfare on the high seas, coasts and rivers has often been overlooked.[49]

---

[48] Anna Pastorek, "Organizacja floty wojennej Republiki Zjednoczonych Prowincji w XVII wieku. Admiralicje, korpus oficerski, załogi," in *Organizacja armii w nowożytnej Europie. Struktura – urzędy – prawo – finance*, ed. Karol Łopatecki (Zabrze: Inforteditions, 2011), 299–311.

[49] Black, *Rethinking Military History*, 159–160.

Chapter VI: The swamps and narrow roads – the landscape

The research on the early modern landscape is a journey into the unknown, where the objects which still exist today are surrounded by some uncertain, vanishing entities. The examination of this theme can be valuable not only for better understanding of the theatre of military operations but also for the general comprehension of the impact of the environmental circumstances on human life.[1] A good example of such observations is the remark made by Michael Roberts, who noted that despite the large size of the sixteenth-century Swedish winter, sleigh travel was faster and easier than travelling in the summer – which not necessarily correspond to our logical but stereotypical beliefs on travelling in the wintertime.[2] In many aspects the environment and landscape of Northern, Central and Eastern Europe has not changed as dramatically as this of Western Europe, and some places look almost the same as in the seventeenth century. The vast majority of rivers in Poland, Norway or Estonia has not been regulated.[3] In Poland, the regulatory process is only now gaining momentum, despite the protests of environmentalists and the European Union bans. Some other features of the landscape made by humans many centuries ago have not changed either – we

---

[1] Brian L. Davies, introduction to *Warfare in Eastern Europe, 1500–1800* (Leiden–Boston: Brill, 2012), 1–2; John Keegan, *Warpaths. Travels of a Military Historian in North America* (London: Pimlico, 1996), 7–11; Jan Tyszkiewicz, "Krajobraz widziany przez historyka", *Krajobrazy Dziedzictwa Narodowego*, no. 1 (2000): 3–6.

[2] Michael Roberts, *The Early Vasas. A History of Sweden, 1523–1611* (Cambridge: Cambridge University Press, 1968), 27.

[3] David Stanners and Philippe Bourdeau, eds., *Europe's Environment. The Dobříš Assessment* (Copenhagen: Office for Official Publications of the European Communities, 1995), 77–79.

can name here strip fields characteristic of Southern Poland or point to a still large number of storks, the best bio-indicators demonstrating clearly the state of pollution.[4] However, a lot was also altered or "modernized "and in particular the great action of drainage of marshlands and swamps in the second half of the twentieth century transformed some areas completely. Most likely the Biebrza Marshes, today the Polish National Park, with its rich wildlife habitats, and a paradise of wetland birds, can give us an idea of the conditions that prevailed in this part of Europe several hundred years ago.

Some places seem unchanged since the Second Northern War, as if abandoned by soldiers only a while ago. Studying carefully the satellite image of the small island Fænø Kalv (which in Danish means "the calf of Fænø" – as the much bigger island Fænø lies in the vicinity) in the strait of the Little Belt – 55° 29' 34.39" N, 9° 39' 35.92" E, we will spot a small Swedish sconce, which looks almost the same as in the days of June 1659 "when the allies drove the Swedes from the mainland, and decided to attack them on the nearby island of Fyn. It was recognized that for this purpose it would be convenient to occupy the small island of Fænø that lies in the middle of the strait, which is not much wider than the range of a musket ball. When the first attack was carried out on the island, the Swedes inflicted great losses to the enemies."[5]

Many such earthworks, hastily built, still exist, just as legends associated with them. Zdzisław Skrok, archaeologist and researcher of Polish cultural landscapes, locates and describes such "Swedish sconces" and other material evidence of the Northern War, which unfortunately may also be easily destroyed.[6] At the level of the military ideas there are also some examples of the persistence of certain technical solutions of the epoch – Swedes first saw the strategic importance of the

---

[4]   Poland has about 50,000 settled stork nests, while Denmark just a few.

[5]   Samuel Pufendorf, *De rebus a Carolo Gustavo Sveciae Rege, gestis commentariorum libri septem, elegantissimis tabulis aeneis exornati cum triplici indice* (Nuremberg 1696), 6: § 10, trans. W.K.

[6]   Zdzisław Skrok, *Wielkie Rozdroże. Ćwiczenia terenowe z archeologii wyobraźni* (Warszawa: Wydawnictwo "Iskry," 2008), 185–190; Zdzisław Skrok, "Zapomniani świadkowie szwedzkich odwiedzin," *Spotkania z zabytkami*, no. 220 (2005): 5–8.

River Narew estuary into the Vistula and constructed a big earthwork on the island in the middle of the stream. Afterwards it was defended for a long time by the Lieutenant Andersson, who collected tribute from the nearby area.[7] Much later, by order of Napoleon, the great and famous fortress of Modlin was built in the years 1807–1812, which also covered the area of the old Swedish fortification.

In Pufendorf's descriptions we will sometimes meet comments on the terrain obstacles which allows us, at least partially, to reconstruct the landscape where the war was fought. Of course in such a vast area: from Finland to Norway and from Jutland to Kraków, there were many different rural and forest landscapes, soils and vegetation types, and the infrastructure like roads, fortifications, or cities were built in accordance with local customs. Certain statements, however, are repeated more often and can possibly be an indication of common features of the landscape, at least for the part of the area which was once the theatre of war.

When it comes to Poland-Lithuania, such remarks frequently concern problems with swamps, marshlands and narrow roads. At the very beginning of the campaign in 1655 near Ujście: "the coming dusk prevented Wittenberg from crossing the river. It seemed quite difficult, because of the broad and deep marshes on both sides of the River Noteć. The Swedes could march only through a narrow path to the dam and the enemy's army was on the opposite bank."[8] The wetlands were also treacherous during rapid retreats, exposing the fleeing to a double threat – of drowning and being caught by the chase. So happened in May 1655, "when the Swedes sent four squadrons of cavalry after the fleeing enemy. They killed a few companies, mostly in the swamps, where the Poles stuck while trying to escape. The Swedes pierced them with bullets from afar."[9] Mud, oxbow lakes, sand dunes and small forests also dominated the area where the great

[7] Samuel Pufendorf, *De rebus a Carolo Gustavo Sveciae Rege, gestis commentariorum libri septem, elegantissimis tabulis aeneis exornati cum triplici indice* (Nuremberg 1696), 2: § 37, trans. W.K.
[8] Pufendorf, *De rebus*, 2: § 15, trans. W.K.
[9] Pufendorf, *De rebus*, 3: § 18, trans. W.K.

battle of Warsaw was fought in the summer of 1656.[10] Such conditions made it difficult to manoeuvre, and in particular to move the artillery. When one of many attacks of the Tatars was rejected: "they suffered a great loss of life and were driven into the marsh, where most of them died. The others jumped from their horses and sought to save themselves on foot."[11]

The complaints about narrow roads are at first not fully understandable. If they were so narrow why did the soldiers not use parallel or nearby trails and tracks, and why did they not go straight through the fields in the rural area? A short action in the autumn of 1656, east of Kraków, when Charles Gustav wanted to stop the Polish relief forces heading for this town may serve as an explanation for difficulties connected with the road network.[12] The Swedes chose a less frequented trail through the foothills of the Carpathian Mountains. They descended from the plateau to the south, where the units had to follow one after the other along a narrow road. It looked more like a ravine, a few metres deep, and was carved into the loess soil by generations of wanderers and farmers. The army could not march through the area parallel to the road, because the passage was barred by the boundaries of small strip fields. However, in the battle of Wojnicz that ensued, the Swedes managed to use the ravine as a trench, stopping the attack of the Polish horse.[13] The road, unchanged except for asphalt pavement, still exists, and is called *Wąwóz Szwedzki – The Swedish Ravine*.[14] Such narrow, muddy roads affected the Swedish army during the retreat in the spring of 1656.

---

[10]   Wiesław Majewski, "Wojna polsko-szwedzka 1655–1660 (potop)." in *Polskie tradycje wojskowe*, vol. 1, ed. Janusz Sikorski (Warszawa, Wydawnictwo Ministerstwa Obrony Narodowej, 1990), 341; Nagielski, *Warszawa 1656* (Warszawa: Bellona SA, 2009), 143.

[11]   Pufendorf, *De rebus*, 3: § 26, trans. W.K.

[12]   Wojciech Krawczuk, "Wojnicz w latach 1655–1660." In *Dzieje Wojnicza od XVI do XVIII wieku*, ed. Wojciech Krawczuk, Piotr Miodunka and Karol Nabiałek (Wojnicz: Towarzystwo Przyjaciół Ziemi Wojnickiej, 2009), 279–283.

[13]   Tadeusz Nowak, "Operacja krakowska 1655," in *Wojna polsko-szwedzka 1655–1660*, ed. Jan Wimmer (Warszawa: Wydawnictwo Ministerstwa Obrony Narodowej, 1973), 235.

[14]   Józef Szymański, *Przewodnik po Wojniczu inaczej* (Wojnicz: Towarzystwo Przyjaciół Ziemi Wojnickiej, 2010), 123.

We have to discuss yet another element of the landscape, venerable and ancient, a descendant of the Old Days. Then, in the first centuries of our era it was known as *Wistlavudu* also the *woods of the Vistula River* where Goths defended their ancient seats against Attila's Huns.[15] In the mid-seventeenth century only fragments of the said vast wilderness left, but forests were abundant and dominant in many regions of this part of Europe. The unique aura and history of the Central European forests still attracts researchers from different disciplines, to wit the books of Simon Shama or Simona Kossak on the Białowieża region.[16]

The forests and woods are quite often mentioned in *De rebus* – as a potential refuge, great place for guerrilla ambush, an obstacle in the march or in the battle.[17] Its importance, however, is not particularly emphasized, since for the Swedes, Poles or Finns it was a familiar environment. It may be noted that Stefan Czarniecki was acclaimed as a very cunning leader in the military actions in dense forests of Southern Poland, particularly at the Battle of Nisko fought on 28th March (New Style) 1656 in the Sandomierz wilderness.[18]

"In the evening, when most of the Swedish horse left the camp to find the fodder, and other regiments dismounted, the sly and quick

---

[15] Probably there was also other name for this ancient forested area – Myrkviðr, although now it is better recognized under the name of Mirkwood. This primeval forest, reminded by J.R.R. Tolkien, really existed and it separated lands belonging to the Goths from those belonging to the Huns. A thesis that *Wistlawudu* and *Myrkviðr* are the same forest area is made more acceptable by one strophe of the ancient poem *Widsith*. We find there a reference to the *Wistlawudu*, also the Vistula woods, where Goths fought the Huns. Of course, this is one of several hypothetical locations of Mirkwood, but quite probable. Wojciech Lipoński, *Narodziny cywilizacji Wysp Brytyjskich* (Poznań: Bene Nati, 1995), 238–240; Rudolf Simek, *Mittelerde. Tolkien und die germanische Mythologie* (München: Verlag C.H. Beck, 2005), 53–54; Gerard Labuda, *Źródła, sagi i legendy do najdawniejszych dziejów Polski* (Warszawa: Państwowe Wydawnictwo Naukowe, 1961), 194.

[16] Simon Schama, *Landscape and Memory* (New York: Vintage Books,1995), 23–53. Simona Kossak, *The Białowieża Forest Saga* (Warsaw: Muza SA, 2001).

[17] Pufendorf, *De rebus*, 2: § 48, 3: § 16, 18, 26, 31, 48, 49.

[18] *There are dense forests in this country...* noted Mikołaj Jemiołowski in his *Diary* describing the fights of Polish peasants with the Swedes. Mikołaj Jemiołowski, *Pamiętnik dzieje Polski zawierający (1648–1679)*, ed. Jan Dzięgielewski (Warszawa: Wydawnictwo DiG, 2000), 181; Andrzej Borcz, *Przemyśl 1656–1657* (Warszawa: Dom Wydawniczy "Bellona," 2006), 20–21, 125.

Czarniecki fell out of the nearby forest with several thousand men, mainly nobles and herded fifty reiters, the outer watch and then the main guard, to the camp." Owing to the vigilance of Charles Gustav, the Swedes managed to repulse the attack. "The King wanted to quickly pursue the enemy, since there was hope to inflict a great defeat on him by the time the foe would escape along the narrow roads. Yet Czarniecki positioned two thousand peasants in the woods, and they started shooting from muskets to the advancing regiments of Douglas. He recognized them as the enemy infantry and attacked, the King went there as well. When he realised that the forces comprised only peasants, the King pursued Czarniecki and Douglas, and after a moderate battle, entered the woods and destroyed over one thousand two hundred peasants, the others scattered in all directions."[19]

The images

An important reason why the work of Pufendorf has been used for centuries is its wonderful, numerous engravings amounting to 128 illustrations drawn up by great artists of the age. The group can be divided thematically into two parts: a smaller one contains thirteen portraits of prominent Swedes of the reign of Charles Gustav, while the greater part consists of one hundred thirteen engravings, specifically images of encounters, cities, fortifications, and state ceremonies. Most illustrations bear also numerous inscriptions and coats of arms. In all the *Seven books* we will find a wide variety of baroque ornaments, panoplies, cartouches, presentations of commemorative medals and coins, as well as various symbols. The importance of the iconographic layer of *De rebus* matches the text and contributes greatly to the popularity of the work.

Most drawings, which constituted a base for the engravings, were delineated by Erik Jönsson Dahlbergh, an artist and renowned spe-

---

[19] Pufendorf, *De rebus*, 3: § 9, trans. W.K.

cialist in the construction of fortifications, who since 1656 accompanied the Swedish army in the field.[20] In recognition of his merits Dahlbergh was ennobled in November 1660. He held later a variety of high military and administrative functions. In the years 1667–1668 he visited Holland and France, where, among other matters he commissioned the above-mentioned engravings. In 1693 he was appointed Swedish Field Marshal. Dahlbergh ended his career as Governor General of Livonia, and administered this province until April 1702, successfully defending it at the beginning of the Great Northern War. He died in 1703 in Stockholm. According to his own reports, adopted by many historians, Dahlbergh distinguished himself particularly in the conquest of Brest-Litovsk in May 1657, and also during the famous crossing of the Little and Big Belts in January 1658. Swedish historians still argue about the actual military achievements of this officer.[21]

But certainly – as Arne Stade revealed – Dahlbergh created a great and valuable collection of texts relating to the Second Northern War. It was Charles Gustav himself who encouraged Dahlberg to prepare a series of drawings depicting his reign. While collecting the sources for the said task, Dahlbergh used very modern methods for his time – including interviews with contemporary witnesses, a few hundred years before the invention of the idea of oral history. His primary objective was, however, the construction of such a vision of the past in which he would play a very significant role and would be shown in the best light. In 1663 the Swedish state bought that collection as valuable for the planned work of commemoration of Charles Gustav, nonetheless, this errand was realized much later in the form of *De rebus*, which appeared in 1696. Samuel Pufendorf readily made use of the collection and especially of the sources presenting the war in

---

[20] Ernst Ericsson, "Dahlbergh Erik Jönsson," in *Svenskt Biografiskt Lexikon*, vol. 9 (Stockholm: Albert Bonniers Förlag, 1931), 615–630. Peter Englund used Dahlbergh as the main character in his books *Ofredsår*, and *Den Oöfvervinnerlige*.

[21] The summary of the ongoing debate, Lars Ericson Wolke, *1658. Tåget över Bält* (Lund: Historiska Media, 2008), 197–202.

Poland, hence it appears to be justified to devote some attention to the said issue.[22]

In publications on Northern and Central Europe in the seventeenth century, the engravings from *Seven books* are used not only as beautiful illustrations but also as good sources for deepening of our understanding of this age. Certainly, they are much better known and popular than the intricate, baroque text of *De rebus*. Yet, although the ability to "see" the past is very attractive, it also poses some risks: the uncritical acceptance of the images, which, after all, are not photographs, and the aforementioned rejection of the text – a less attractive medium, as indicated by the historians from Johan Huizinga to Francis Haskell.[23]

The basic reference to Dahlbergh's vast legacy is the book of Börje Magnusson, in which he presented a detailed analysis of the style and skills of the artist, but deliberately avoided the issue of the documentary value of the drawings.[24]

The illustrations and the reality

With all the richness of detail, we need to ask to what extent the images faithfully reflect the reality, how they were created and on what basis. Dahlbergh's artistic skill is undisputed, but long since we know about his methods of creating pictures so as to meet the tastes and demands of his patrons. A good example is his another, monumental work *Suecia antiqua et hodierna*, in which, at the request of the authorities, Dahlbergh demonstrated palaces, cities and histori-

---

[22] Arne Stade, *Erik Dahlbergh och Carl Gustafs krigshistoria. Carl X Gustaf – studier* 3 (Kristianstad: Militärhistoriska Fraget, 1967), 11–25, 143–217.

[23] Francis Haskell, *History and its Images. Art and the Interpretation of the Past* (New Haven–London: Yale University Press, 1995), 493–495.

[24] Börje Magnusson, *Att illustrera fäderneslandet – en studie i Erik Dahlberghs verksamhet som tecknare*. Acta Universitatis Upsaliensis, Ars Suetica 10 (Uppsala 1986), 48–76, 258.

cal sites of Sweden.[25] It had to be the best possible presentation of the then so powerful Kingdom. However, and not seldom, the artist drew buildings that existed only in plans, and were yet to be built. It could happen that if a real perspective of some place was distorted, the artist made some slight or radical shifts to create the proper, aesthetic space.

The problem of the documentary value of the images is particularly important and discussed in Poland. As a result of massive destruction, especially of World War II, the cultural heritage of architecture largely ceased to exist in our country. The time of rebuilding, especially of the Old Town of the capital – Warsaw, contributed greatly to the development of the research in the field of architectural history. Every track of the past, every source was of utmost importance, and the Dahlbergh's drawings are in many cases the oldest existing images of many Polish towns, especially the smaller ones. Paradoxically, a work commemorating Charles Gustav, the king-destroyer, has been useful in the reconstruction of the cultural landscape, which he himself and his army partially obliterated. The artist had a good feeling for the characteristic features of the environs he drew. The great, bent, wooden wayside cross with a characteristic roof, in the foreground of the engraving "The crossing by Zakroczym in 1657" represents a sign which was, until recently, a typical, dominant element of the Polish rural landscape, which Dahlbergh noticed and utilized in his picture.[26]

A significant part of the drawings was sketched by Dahlbergh himself, but he also used various different sources – the works of other artists. Unfortunately only an insignificant part of them has been identified.[27] The note "Dahlbergh ad vivum delineavit" – "Dahlbergh

---

[25] Magdalena Gram, *Historien om Suecia…*, http://www.kb.se/samlingarna/oversikt/suecia/historien-om-sucecia/ [4 June 2014].

[26] Such symbols were absent in the Swedish landscape, since they were completely destroyed during the Reformation, after the Riksdag in Västerås in 1544. Werner Buchholz, "Schweden mit Finnland," in *Dänemark, Norwegen und Schweden im Zeitalter der Reformation und Konfessionalisierung, Nordische Königreiche und Konfession 1500 bis 1660*, ed. Matthias Asche, Anton Schindling (Münster: Aschendorff Verlag, 2003), 190.

[27] Magnusson, *Att illustrera fäderneslandet*, 50–52.

drew from nature," appearing on many illustrations may be misleading, as, not infrequently, it does not match the artist's itinerary.

An important text for the appropriate presentation of the Dahlbergh's work is the book of Bronisław Heyduk and Adam Przyboś. Not only did the authors discuss the artistic and historic dimensions of his drawings, but also presented a large part of his *Diary*, from the years 1656–1657, also when the artist stayed in Poland.[28] This thorough yet accessible work has awakened an interest in the pictures. On the basis of the existing literature it can be stated that in respect of the documentary value, the engravings can be clearly divided into two distinct groups.

The first, smaller one, is composed of illustrations which, according to all the studies, reflect the reality very faithfully. Bogusław Dybaś points out that in some cases the illustrations give a true and fair view of fortifications built just before, or already during the war.[29]

The best example is the famous view of Warsaw in the year 1656, seen from the town of Praga, located on the opposite bank of the Vistula River. It is considered a *paramount source* for the research on Warsaw in the age of the Vasa dynasty.[30] Even the smallest details of the landscape were captured perfectly by the artist, to wit a small, old, ruined rampart made of earth at the foot of *Villa Regia* – the King's Palace, known also under the name of Casimir's Palace.[31] Freehand drawing of Dahlbergh, which was the basis for the engraving, is preserved in the collection of the Kungliga Biblioteket in Stockholm.[32] Nevertheless, even in the case of such meticulously researched en-

---

[28] Bronisław Heyduk and Adam Przyboś, *Dahlbergh w Polsce. Dziennik i ryciny szwedzkie z dziejów "Potopu" 1656–1657* (Wrocław: Zakład Narodowy im. Ossolińskich – Wydawnictwo, 1971).

[29] It is the case of Dünaburg or Brest Lithovsk. Bogusław Dybaś, *Fortece Rzeczypospolitej. Studium z dziejów budowy fortyfikacji stałych* (Toruń: Towarzystwo Naukowe w Toruniu, 1998), 201, footnote 218.

[30] Ryszard Mączyński, "Zarys dziejów badań nad zabytkami Warszawy," in *Katalog Zabytków Sztuki. Miasto Warszawa*, part 1: *Stare Miasto*, ed. Jerzy Z. Łoziński, Andrzej Rottermund (Warszawa: Wydawnictwa Artystyczne i Filmowe, 1993), 3, 30.

[31] Lech Królikowski, *Warszawa – dzieje fortyfikacji* (Warszawa: Wydawnictwo "Trio," 2011), 83–85.

[32] Magnusson, *Att illustrera fäderneslandet*, 74; Heyduk, Przyboś, *Dahlbergh w Polsce*, 191.

graving, there are still some unresolved questions. The art historian Jakub Sito finds it imperative to examine: whether Dahlbergh used the instrument of *camera obscura,* the ancestor of the photo camera. The confirmation of such a presumption would add a new meaning to the image.[33] Could it be a "photograph" after all?

Most likely, the drawing of the town of Brest–Litovsk was very accurate too, but the problem here is somewhat different. The town was destroyed and rebuilt so many times that it would be practically unfeasible to prove such a claim, even if some research possibilities exist, as demonstrated by the studies of Karol Łopatecki.[34]

Another, but still different example, is a detailed plan of the fortress called Głowa Gdańska (*Danziger Haupt*). The Swedes surrendered it in December 1659. In this case Dahlbergh used a commemorative medal sculpted by Johan Höhn der Jüngere as a model for a draft. It was ordered in April 1660 by the burghers of Gdańsk, who in this manner wanted to celebrate a significant victory over the army of Charles Gustav.[35]

The second group consists of illustrations in which reality is mixed with fantasy. The problem is that we cannot reject them entirely, as they contain valuable information that need to be separated, and besides, the fantasies also have their value. Dahlbergh struggled for instance with great difficulties while drawing a view of the siege of Kraków, the ancient capital of the Kingdom of Poland, conducted in 1656. He used a variety of sources: the picture from the *Civitates or-*

---

[33] Jakub Sito, "Dahlbergh i inni. O szwedzkich rysownikach – weducistach doby wojennej w Polsce i ich dziele," in *Po obu stronach Bałtyku. Wzajemne relacje między Skandynawią a Europą Środkową. On the Opposite Sides of the Baltic Sea. Relations between Scandinavian and Central European Countries*, vol. 2, ed. Jan Harasimowicz et al. (Wrocław: Wydawnictwo "Via Nova," 2006), 514–515.

[34] Karol Łopatecki: "Między włoską a holenderską sztuką fortyfikacyjną. Plan rozbudowy Brześcia Litewskiego w świetle 'Geometrich Plan der Statt Brzesche in Littawen' z 1657 roku," in *Zapiski Historyczne*, vol. 74, part 4 (2009), 77–94; "Fortyfikacje Brześcia Litewskiego w dobie II wojny północnej," in *Studia i Materiały do Historii Wojskowości*, vol. 43 (2007), 159–176; "Prace kartograficzne wykonane na ziemiach Rzeczypospolitej przez szwedzkich inżynierów wojskowych w XVII stuleciu," in *Studia i Materiały do Historii Wojskowości*, vol. 46 (2009), 55–80.

[35] Maria Stahr, *Medale Wazów w Polsce, 1587–1668* (Wrocław: Zakład Narodowy im. Ossolińskich, 1990), 175–177.

bis terrarum by Georg Braun and Frans Hogenberg, the drawings of Matthias Palbitzki, notwithstanding, the end result was far from satisfactory.[36] Maciej Ziemierski notes, however, that some topographical details and in particular the water network were drawn in accordance with the actual situation, hence the picture is not completely deprived of epistemic value.[37]

A similar situation occurs in the case of the plan and the view of Gdańsk – both are placed on one engraving. The plan is extremely precise and rich in details, while the view of the town, depicted on a narrow strip at the top of the engraving, is full of errors and disarray. Jerzy Stankiewicz, expert on the fortifications of Gdańsk, states that the artist did not even bother to collate these two drawings.[38] Basically, the Swedish maps, prepared by experts from the engineering troops, are much more accurate than the townscapes.

The illustrations of De rebus, however, still contain a lot of mysteries. Paweł Nowakowski, who has recently studied a veduta of the small town of Iłża, has found that the picture reflects a state of affairs before the year 1617. Did the artist use some lost image of the place? Why did he commence to draw Iłża at all – which was not particularly important during the war?[39]

On 26th June (Old Style) 1657, the retreating Swedish army under the command of the King reached the castle of Złotów (Flatau) near the Polish border. Charles Gustav decided to attack this fortified place and it was his last victory before leaving Poland.[40] The castle was destroyed and burnt. This victory was immortalized by Dahlbergh on the engraving with two images of two fortifications – the inscriptions record that it is the view of Złotów and the plan of Stare Drawsko (Draheim). Problematic, though, is the size of the castle in Złotów, it seems just too big for the limited space where it once ex-

---

[36] Magnusson, Att illustrera fäderneslandet, 63; Maciej Ziemierski, "Widok szwedzkiego oblężenia Krakowa w 1655 r. autorstwa Erika Jönssona Dahlbergha, kwestie interpretacji," in Krzysztofory, vol. 22 (Kraków 2004), 37–41.

[37] Ziemierski, "Widok," 40.

[38] Stankiewicz, "System fortyfikacyjny Gdańska," 77–78.

[39] Paweł Nowakowski, Iłża. Miasto kościelne (Radom: Neoflam, 2012), 93–102.

[40] Pufendorf, De rebus, 4: § 20, trans. W.K.

isted. Or maybe it was "inflated" a bit by Dahlbergh, as it was after all the last victory of the King in the Polish campaign? Another hypothetical explanation is that it is the plan and the view of one place, i.e. Stare Drawsko, where the old castle and the bastion fortifications were actually quite large.[41]

There is, therefore, no good answer to the question whether the drawings accurately reflect the actual situation. Each image requires a separate analysis of the individual elements. The richness of truthful information can also be found in the staffage, e.g. small figures of the second or third plan present a rich variety of clothes, accessories and weapons.

---

[41] Jerzy Stankiewicz, "Ze studiów nad fortyfikacjami pruskimi na ziemiach polskich," in *Studia i Materiały do Historii Wojskowości*, vol. 12, part 1 (1966), 110.

Afterthoughts

The *Seven books*, Samuel Pufendorf's monumental work on the reign of Charles Gustav and Second Northern War, printed in 1696, still retains its value. It is not just about the participation of Pufendorf in the events he later described, or that he knew many outstanding commanders and high-ranking dignitaries of the epoch. For obvious reasons no historian will ever acquire such intimate knowledge of the said matters. The great strength of the book lies also in the synthetic evaluation of all the important theatres of war, either military or diplomatic. In this great, Pan-European conflict, Sweden was at the centre of the struggle, which naturally presents us with a broad perspective. Therefore, not only does *De rebus* retain the information concerning the course of events in Stockholm, London, Warsaw or Copenhagen, but also descriptions of the developments in Ghana or Constantinople. Ergo the book still remains an important reference.

Undeniably, we have a large number of more detailed and modern studies at our disposal. Most often, however, they will cover only a single event. Assembling all these fragments together would certainly give a great result, but overcoming language difficulties and combining diverse, national and historiographical traditions is a somewhat difficult, if not an unfeasible task – although it must be stressed that especially in the field of military and history of diplomacy we have some interesting proposals, to name the works of Peter Englund, Yaroslaw Fedoruk, Robert I. Frost, Mirosław Nagielski or Henadz Sahanovich (alphabetical order).

Yet the work of Pufendorf cannot be accepted easily and without reservation, as it still hides a lot of mysteries and is not devoid of flaws. This is primarily due to the author's process of writing, his specific use of historical sources. Sometimes he exploited unique documents from the archives, but at times he was content with mere copying of some printed texts into his book. Certainly he worked quickly, which does not allow absolute concentration on each sentence. It is not always easy to check his sources, as some documents perished or certain facts are inconsistent with other accounts. However, when comparing Pufendorf's stories with the results of the most recent research, we also perceive that his old text still retains its validity, and what is more, it can add some new elements to our perception of the epoch.

Such a method of writing produces also, probably unintentional, but nevertheless, impressive end result. Pufendorf did not have much time to carefully analyze and reshape so many sources. Often, he merged them to form one piece. The author's comments are rare, and we read about the events as if it was not clear what happened later, as the issues were probably seen by the contemporaries, participants of struggles, when the outcome was still uncertain. He did not write "a story of a courtier–flatterer." In *Seven Books* there is a lot of criticism about politics of Charles Gustav. It is sometimes hidden, but at times open. The rations of opponents and enemies of the King are presented carefully, they are often more convincing than the arguments used by the Swedish side.

It is clearly evident that Pufendorf was far more engrossed in the activities of diplomats and secretaries than these of generals. As a result, *Seven books* are not only a vivid description of bloody campaigns, but a unique and thorough analysis of the "diplomatic war," with many details about the specificity of various chanceries. As the auxiliary sciences of history are faced with a serious crisis, mainly due to the reduction of the available courses, any support in explaining this subject is much needed. The free access to the Swedish archives allowed the author to utilize abundant reports, letters and treaties. Pufendorf as a historian worked in favourable conditions for the epoch, which combined with his critical approach to the sources yielded excellent results.

The King of Sweden, Charles XI and senior officials showed great confidence in historiographer Samuel Pufendorf. It seems that trying to write an objective and sometimes critical book on Charles Gustav, the author did not disappoint their expectations, offered remarkable testimony of his skills and confirmed aspirations of the Swedish authorities of the early modern age. Somewhat contradicting the previous sentence, there is also the vague suspicion that only few people read the entire voluminous tome.

In turn, rich and detailed illustrations of the work remain extraordinary, yet not fully explored. While Erik Dahlbergh as artist is renowned and appreciated, still a fundamental question about the documentary value of his works goes unanswered. This, however, requires creation of a large, interdisciplinary project. Dahlbergh's illustrations resemble the text of Pufendorf – they are a mixture of different elements of varying values, and of unique information, at times, though, they are simple fantasies or themes "borrowed" from other sources.

In many modern analysis of the Second Northern War we encounter considerations of technological superiority of one or the other side in the conflict. There were as yet no tanks or aircraft in the mid-seventeenth century, but for many military historians the "invincible" heavy hussars – or equally "unstoppable" Swedish infantry are very tempting replacements of these modern weapons. While there is nothing wrong in such analyses, they may also be distributed improperly, consequently, we will forget that the *husaria* units were few in the said war, or that the Swedish horse was also present on the battlefields. Pufendorf, unencumbered by the fascination with weaponry and the technological paradigm, presents a different perspectives on war: from the *face of battle* to the strategic level. This does not mean, however, that in *De rebus* there is no information relating to the technically difficult proceedings. A good example is the diverse ability of the warring sides to deal with many water hazards. Such "combined operations" of the land forces on the water serve as a very good indicator of the skills of the officers and soldiers likewise. Both the crossing of the frozen Belt straits, the escape from the Vistula–San bifurcation, and the landing of the allied forces on the island of Als provide us with the compelling evidence that the combatants were usually highly skilled.

The multi-threaded story of *De rebus* includes topics, which have not been clarified so far, or, that do not comply with generally accepted theses. Sometimes the author was wrong, sometimes he had to yield to the outside pressure of a rancorous magnate or the Swedish Crown officials. Notwithstanding, he managed to raise thorny questions.

Many issues, mentioned briefly in *De rebus*, remain unexplored. We would like to learn more about the Jewish defenders of the town of Przemyśl in 1657, they were still *a few companies strong*. One would like to read a play prepared by the Catholic priests and performed at the fair in the Silesian town of Nysa about the supposed death of Charles X Gustav in the battle of Nowy Dwór. War propaganda of all the sides is the subject which lingers in the shadow of the battles. How far did the arrangements for the coronation of Charles Gustav as the King of Poland in Warsaw in 1655 go? And so forth. There are still numerous fascinating fireside tales from the time of the Northern War to be told.

Bibliography

Quoted Works of Samuel Pufendorf

Pufendorf, Samuel. *De rebus a Carolo Gustavo Sveciae Rege, gestis commentariorum libri septem, elegantissimis tabulis aeneis exornati cum triplici indice.* Nuremberg: 1696.

———. *Sieben Bücher von denen Thaten Carls Gustavs, Königs in Schweden mit vortrefflichen Kupfern ausgezieret und mit nötigen Registern versehen.* Translated by Samuel Rodigast. Nuremberg: Christoph Riegel, 1697.

———. *Histoire du Regne de Charles Gustave, Roy de Svede comprise en sept commentaries, enrichis de tailles douces, traduite en francois sur le latin, de monsieur le baron Samuel de Pufendorf, avec trois indices.* Anonymous translation. Nuremberg: Christoph Riegel, 1697.

———. *Sju böcker om konung Carl X Gustafs bragder.* Translated by Adolf Hillman. Stockholm: Wahlström & Widstrand, 1912–15.

———. *Siedem ksiąg o czynach Karola Gustawa, króla Szwecji.* Translated and edited by Wojciech Krawczuk. Warszawa: Wydawnictwo DiG, 2013.

———. *Einleitung zu der Historie der vornehmsten Reiche und Staaten.* Frankfurt am Main: 1682.

———. *Commentariorum de rebus Suecicis libri XXVI ab expeditione Gustavi Adolfi Regis in Germaniam ab abdicationem usque Christinae.* Duisburg: 1686.

———. *De rebus gestis Friderici Wilhelmi Magni, electoris Brandenburgici, commentariorum libri novendecim,* Berlin: 1695.

———. *Gesammelte Werke,* vol. 1: *Briefwechsel.* Edited by Detlef Döring. Berlin: Akademie Verlag, 1996.

———. *The Present State of Germany.* Translated by Edmund Bohun. Edited and with Introduction by Michael J. Seidler. Indianapolis, IN: Liberty Fund, 2007.

Printed Sources

Ascheberg, Rutger von. *Fältmarskalken Rutger von Ascheberg Journal och korrespondens till år 1680.* Edited by Alf Åberg. Stockholm 1951. Kungl. Samfundet för utgifvande af handskrifter rörande Skandinaviens historia. Historiska handlingar del 34: 1.

Bibliotheca Historica Sveo-Gothica; eller förteckning uppå så väl trykte som handskrifne Böcker, Tractater och Skrifter, hvilka handla om Svenska Historien, eller därutinnan kunna gifva Ljus; Med Critiska och historiska Anmärkningar, part 9. Edited by Carl Gustaf Warmholtz. Uppsala: 1803.

Czepko, Christian. *Schwedische Reise, Swedish Journey*. With Introduction by Joanna Lamparska, English translation by Anna Bielawska. Świdnica: Parafia Ewangelicko-Augsburska pw. św. Trójcy, 2008.

Dyaryusze sejmowe r 1585 (The Diaries of the 1585 Diet). Edited by Aleksander Czuczyński. Kraków: Akademia Umiejętności, 1901. Scriptores Rerum Polonicarum, vol. 18.

Jemiołowski, Mikołaj. *Pamiętnik dzieje Polski zawierający (1648–1679)*. Edited by Jan Dzięgielewski. Warszawa: Wydawnictwo DiG, 2000.

Łoś, Jakub. *Pamiętnik towarzysza chorągwi pancernej*. Edited by Romuald Śreniawa-Szypiowski. Warszawa: Wydawnictwo DiG, 2000.

Radziwiłł, Albrycht Stanisław. *Pamiętnik*. Edited and translated by Adam Przyboś and Roman Żelewski, vol. 1–3. Warszawa: Państwowy Instytut Wydawniczy, 1980.

Ranotowicz, Stefan. *Opisanie inkursji Szwedów do Polski do Krakowa (1655–1657)*. Edited by Józef Mitkowski. Kraków: Towarzystwo Miłośników Historii i Zabytków Krakowa, 1958.

Res Polonicae ex Archivo Regni Daniae, 2 pars. Edited by Carolina Lanckorońska et Georgius Steen Jensen. Roma: Institutum Historicum Polonicum Romae, 1969. Elementa ad fontium editiones, vol. 20.

Swedish Diplomats at Cromwell's Court. The Missions of Peter Julius Coyet and Christer Bonde. Translated and edited by Michael Roberts. London: Royal Historical Society, 1988.

Terlon Hugues de. *Memoires de Chevalier de Terlon. Pour rendre compte au Roy, de ses Négociations, depuis l'année 1656 jusqu'en 1661. Tome premier. Suivant la Copie Imprimé à Paris Chez Louis Billaine*. Paris: Barbin 1682.

Volumina Legum, vol. 2. Edited by Jozafat Ohryzko. Petersburg: 1859.

Secondary Works

Asker, Björn. *Karl X Gustav: en biografi*. Lund: Historiska Media, 2010.

Augusiewicz, Sławomir. *Działania militarne w Prusach Książęcych w latach 1656–1657*. Olsztyn: Ośrodek Badań Naukowych im. Wojciecha Kętrzyńskiego w Olsztynie, 1999.

Ånimmer, Lena. "Ett krigsbyte från 1658." In *När sundet blev gräns. Till minne av Roskildefreden, Årsbok för Riksarkivet och landsarkiven 2008*, 45–50. Växjö 2008.

Baranowski, Bohdan. "Tatarszczyzna wobec wojny polsko-szwedzkiej w latach 1655–1660." In *Polska w okresie drugiej wojny północnej 1655–1660*, vol. 1, edited by Kazimierz Lepszy, 453–489. Warszawa: Państwowe Wydawnictwo Naukowe, 1957.

Barwiński, Edward, Ludwik Birkenmajer, and Jan Łoś. *Sprawozdanie z poszukiwań w Szwecji dokonanych z ramienia Akademii Umiejętności.* Kraków: Akademia Umiejętności, 1914.

Bennich-Björkman, Bo. *Författaren i ämbetet. Studier i funktion och organisation av författarämbeten vid svenska hovet och kansliet 1550–1850.* Uppsala: 1970. Studia Litterarum Upsaliensia 5.

Black, Jeremy. *Rethinking Military History.* New York: Routledge, 2008.

Bogdanowski, Janusz. *Sztuka obronna (Defensive Art in the Landscape of the Cracow Jura).* Kraków: Zarząd Jurajskich Parków Krajobrazowych w Krakowie, 1993.

Borcz, Andrzej. *Przemyśl 1656–1657.* Warszawa: Dom Wydawniczy "Bellona," 2006.

Braudy, Leo. *From Chivalry to Terrorism. War and the Changing Nature of Masculinity.* New York: Alfred A. Knopf, 2003.

Brzezinski, Richard, and Angus McBride. *Polish Armies 1569–1696.* London: Osprey Publishing, 1987. Man-at-Arms Series of Osprey, no. 184 and 188 (vol. 1 and 2).

Buchholz, Werner. "Schweden mit Finnland." In *Dänemark, Norwegen und Schweden im Zeitalter der Reformation und Konfessionalisierung, Nordische Königreiche und Konfession 1500 bis 1660,* edited by Matthias Asche and Anton Schindling, 107–243. Münster: Aschendorff Verlag, 2003.

Burke, Peter. *The Fabrication of Louis XIV.* New Haven–London: Yale University Press, 1992.

Childs, John. *Warfare in the Seventeenth Century.* Washington: Smithsonian Books, 2004. Smithsonian History of Warfare.

Chorążyczewski, Waldemar. "Początki kancelarii pokojowej za Jagiellonów." In *Polska kancelaria królewska. Między władzą a społeczeństwem,* part 3, edited by Waldemar Chorążyczewski and Wojciech Krawczuk, 33–46. Warszawa: Wydawnictwo DiG, 2008.

Chorążyczewski, Waldemar, and Agnieszka Rosa. "Samoświadectwa pracowników polskiej kancelarii królewskiej czasów nowożytnych. Przypadek sekretarza królewskiego Jana Piotrowskiego." In *Polska kancelaria królewska. Między władzą a społeczeństwem,* part 4, edited by Waldemar Chorążyczewski and Wojciech Krawczuk, 87–105. Warszawa: Wydawnictwo DiG, 2011.

Chróścicki, Juliusz. *Sztuka i polityka. Funkcje propagandowe sztuki za Wazów 1587–1668 (Art and Politics 1587–1668).* Warszawa: Państwowe Wydawnictwo Naukowe, 1983.

Cieślak, Edmund. "Okres 'potopu' szwedzkiego." In *Historia Gdańska,* vol. 3, edited by Edmund Cieślak, 36–56. Gdańsk: Instytut Historii Polskiej Akademii Nauk, Zakład Historii Gdańska i Dziejów Morskich Polski, 1993.

Czaika, Otfried. "Carolus Redivivus oder der wiederaufwachende nordische Löwe – das Bild Karl XII. als Retter des Protestantismus in der proschwedischen Publizistik." In *Religia i polityka. Kwestie wyznaniowe i konflikty polityczne w Europie w XVIII wieku. W 300. rocznicę konwencji w Altranstädt*, edited by Lucyna Harc and Gabriela Wąs, 57–83. Wrocław: Wydawnictwo Uniwersytetu Wrocławskiego, 2009.

Czapliński, Władysław. "Projekt utworzenia floty kaperskiej w czasie 'potopu' szwedzkiego." *Rocznik Gdański*, vol. 13 (1954): 131–132.

Dahlgren, Erik Wilhelm. "Louis de Geer." In *Svenskt Biografiskt Lexikon*, vol. X, 457–476. Stockholm: Albert Bonniers Förlag, 1931.

Dahlgren, Stellan. "Karl X Gustav." In *Svenskt Biografiskt Lexikon*, vol. 20, 641–643. Stockholm 1973–1975.

Davis, Brain L. "Introduction." In *Warfare in Eastern Europe, 1500–1800*, 1–17. Leiden–Boston: Brill, 2012.

Davies, Paul. "That Mysterious Flow." *Scientific American*, no. 287 (September 2002): 40–47.

Dąbrowski, Janusz. *Senat koronny. Stan sejmujący w czasach Jana Kazimierza*. Kraków: Historia Iagellonica, 2000.

Deventer, Jörg. "Protestant Self-Assertion in Silesia after the Peace of Westphalia: The Journey of Christian Czepko from Świdnica to Stockholm (1654/1655)." In *Po obu stronach Bałtyku. Wzajemne relacje między Skandynawią a Europą Środkową. On the Opposite Sides of the Balic Sea. Relations between Scandinavian and Central European Countries*, edited by Jan Harasimowicz, Piotr Oszczanowski, Marcin Wisłocki, vol. 1, 115–120. Wrocław: Wydawnictwo "Via Nova," 2006.

Döring, Detlef. *Pufendorf Studien: Beiträge zur Biographie Samuel von Pufendorfs und zu seiner Entwicklung als Historiker und theologischer Schriftsteller*. Berlin: Duncker & Humblot, 1992.

———. "Die Privatbibliothek Samuel Pufendorfs." *Zentralblatt für Bibliothekwesen*, vol. 104, part 3 (1990): 102–112.

Droste, Heiko. "Schwedische Korrespondenz über Polen am Beispiel Heinrich von Schöllens, Kommissar in Breslau von 1664–1666." In *Po obu stronach Bałtyku. Wzajemne relacje między Skandynawią a Europą Środkową. On the Opposite Sides of the Baltic Sea. Relations between Scandinavian and Central European Countries*, edited by Jan Harasimowicz, Piotr Oszczanowski, Marcin Wisłocki, vol. 1, 121–130. Wrocław: Wydawnictwo "Via Nova," 2006.

Dybaś, Bogusław. *Fortece Rzeczypospolitej. Studium z dziejów budowy fortyfikacji stałych w państwie polsko-litewskim w XVII wieku*. Toruń: Towarzystwo Naukowe w Toruniu, 1998.

Ekdahl, Sven. *Grunwald 1410*. Kraków: Avalon, 2010.

Englund, Peter. *Ofredsår. Om den svenska stormaktstiden och en man i dess mitt*. Stockholm: Atlantis, 2001.

———. *Den oövervinnerlige. Om de svenska stormaktstiden och en man i dess mitt*. Stockholm: Atlantis, 2000.

Eriksson, Bo. *Lützen 1632. Et ödesdigert beslut.* Stockholm: Norstedts, 2006.

Ericsson, Ernst. "Dahlbergh Erik Jönsson." In *Svenskt Biografiskt Lexikon*, vol. 9, 615–630. Stockholm: Albert Bonniers Förlag, 1931.

Stanners, David, and Philippe Bourdeau, eds. *Europes Environment. The Dobříš Assessment.* Copenhagen: Office for Official Publications of the European Communities, 1995.

Fedoruk, Yaroslav. *Wilens'kyj dogowir 1656 roku. Schidnoewropejs'ka kriza i Ukraina u seredyni XVII stolittja (The Treaty of Vilnius (1656). The East European Crisis and Ukraine in the Mid-Seventeenth Century).* Kiev: "Kyiv-Mohyla Academy" Publishing House, 2011.

Forssberg, Anna Maria. "Att hålla folket på got humor. Informationsspridning, krigspropaganda och mobilisering i Sverige 1655–1680," *Acta Universitatis Stockholmiensis. Stockholm Studies in History*, vol. 80 (2005).

Franken, Martinus Antonius Maria. "The General Tendencies and Structural Aspects of the Foreign Policy and Diplomacy of the Dutch Republic in the Latter Half of the 17th Century." *Acta Historiae Nerlandica*, vol. 3 (1968): 1–42.

Frost, Robert I. *The Northern Wars. War, State and Society in Northeastern Europe, 1558–1721.* Harlow: Longman, 2000.

———. *After the Deluge. Poland – Lithuania and the Second Northern War 1655–1660.* Cambridge: Cambridge University Press, 1993.

Gierowski, Józef Andrzej. *The Polish-Lithuanian Commonwealth in the XVIIIth Century. From Anarchy to Well Organized State.* Kraków: Polska Akademia Umiejętności, 1996.

———. *Rzeczpospolita w dobie złotej wolności (1648–1763).* Kraków: Oficyna Wydawnicza "Fogra," 2001.

Glete, Jan. *Swedish Naval Administration, 1521–1721. Resource Flows and Organisational Capabilities.* Leiden: Brill, 2010.

Göransson, Sven. *Den europeiska konfessionspolitikens upplösning: 1654–1660: Religion och utrikespolitik under Karl X Gustav.* Uppsala–Wiesbaden: Uppsala Universitets Årsskrift, 1956.

Granlund, Victor G. *En svensk koloni i Afrika: eller svenska afrikanska kompaniets historia.* Stockholm: Norstedt, 1879.

Groth, Andrzej. "Czasy Rzeczypospolitej szlacheckiej." In *Historia Pucka*, 91–207. Gdańsk: Wydawnictwo "Marpress," 1998.

Haskell, Francis. *History and Its Images. Art and the Interpretation of the Past.* New Haven–London: Yale University Press, 1995.

Hellerstedt, Andreas. *Ödets teater. Ödesföreställningar i Sverige vid 17–hundra talets början.* Lund: Nordic Academic Press, 2009.

Heyduk, Bronisław, and Adam Przyboś. *Dahlbergh w Polsce. Dziennik i ryciny szwedzkie z dziejów "Potopu" 1656–1657.* Wrocław: Zakład Narodowy imienia Ossolińskich – Wydawnictwo, 1971.

Herzig, Arno. "Die Rezeption Gustav Adolfs in Schlesien." In *Po obu stronach Bałtyku. Wzajemne relacje między Skandynawią a Europą Środkową. On the Opposite Sides of the Baltic Sea. Relations between Scandinavian and Central European Countries*, edited by Jan Harasimowicz, Piotr Oszczanowski and Marcin Wisłocki, vol. 1, 63–68. Wrocław: Wydawnictwo "Via Nova," 2006.

Holm, Torsten. *Översikt över Sveriges krig under 1600-talets senare hälvt*. Stockholm: Militärlitteraturföreningens förlag, 1927.

Hoppe, Klaus. "Die Greuel des Krieges." In *30jähriger Krieg, Münster und der Westfälische Frieden*, vol. 1, 145–166. Münster: Stadtmuseum Münster, 1998.

Isacson, Claes-Göran. *Karl X Gustavs krig. Fälttågen i Polen, Tyskland, Baltikum, Danmark och Sverige 1655–1660*. Lund: Historiska Media, 2004.

Katelaar, Eric. "Documents as monuments." *Archeion*, vol. 62 (2011): 51–63.

Keegan, John. *Warpaths. Travels of a Military Historian in North America*. London: Pimlico, 1996.

Kennedy Grimsted, Patricia. *The "Lithuanian Metrica" in Moscow and Warsaw. Reconstructing the Archives of the Grand Duchy of Lithuania*. Cambridge, MA: Published for the Harvard Ukrainian Research Institute, Harvard University, by Oriental Research Partners, 1984.

Kersten, Adam. *Pierwszy opis obrony Jasnej Góry w 1655 r.* Warszawa: Książka i Wiedza, 1959.

———. *Stefan Czarniecki 1599–1665*. Warszawa: Wydawnictwo Ministerstwa Obrony Narodowej, 1963.

———. *Sienkiewicz* – Potop – *historia*. Warszawa: Państwowy Instytut Wydawniczy, 1974.

———. *Hieronim Radziejowski. Studium władzy i opozycji*. Warszawa: Państwowy Instytut Wydawniczy, 1988.

Kossak, Simona. *The Białowieża Forest Saga*. Warszawa: Muza SA, 2001.

Krawczuk, Wojciech. *Metryka Koronna za Zygmunta III Wazy*. Kraków: Uniwersytet Jagielloński, 1995.

———. *Metrykanci koronni. Rozwój registratury centralnej od XVI do XVIII wieku* (*The Polish Crown Chancery Metricants. The Development of Crown Chancery Records from Sixteenth to Eighteenth Century*). Kraków: Historia Iagellonica, 2002.

———. "Wojnicz w latach 1655–1660." In *Dzieje Wojnicza od XVI do XVIII wieku*, edited by Wojciech Krawczuk, Piotr Miodunka and Karol Nabiałek, 275–283. Wojnicz: Towarzystwo Przyjaciół Ziemi Wojnickiej, 2009.

———. "O Rochu Kowalskim i Tatarach." In *Inter majestatem ac libertatem. Studia z dziejów nowożytnych dedykowane Profesorowi Kazimierzowi Przybosiowi*, edited by Jarosław Stolicki, Marek Ferenc and Janusz Dąbrowski, 121–127. Kraków: Historia Iagellonica, 2010.

————. "Kancelaria pokojowa za Wazów." In *Polska kancelaria królewska. Między władzą a społeczeństwem*, part 3, edited by Waldemar Chorążyczewski and Wojciech Krawczuk, 47–54. Warszawa: Wydawnictwo DiG, 2008.

————. "Uwagi Samuela Pufendorfa o praktykach kancelaryjnych w XVII wieku." In *Polska kancelaria królewska. Między władzą a społeczeństwem*, part 4, edited by Waldemar Chorążyczewski and Wojciech Krawczuk, 107–115. Warszawa: Wydawnictwo DiG, 2011.

————. "The Sources on the Early Modern Livonia in the Polish Crown Chancery Books. The first years of Sigismund III Vasa's reign." *Latvijas Vēstures Institūta Žurnālis*, no. 83 (2012): 89–97.

Królikowski, Lech. *Warszawa – dzieje fortyfikacji*. Warszawa: Wydawnictwo "Trio," 2011.

Kubala, Ludwik. *Wojna szwecka w roku 1655 i 1656*. Lwów: Biblioteka Historyczna Altenberga, 1880.

Kubala, Ludwik. *Wojna brandenburska i najazd Rakoczego w roku 1656 i 1657*. Lwów–Warszawa: Biblioteka Historyczna Altenberga, 1917.

Kulakovs'kyj, Petro. *Kancelarija ruśkoj (wołyńśkoj) Metryki 1569–1683 rr. Studija z istorii ukrainśkogo regionalizmu w Reczi Pospolitij* (*Chancery of the Ruthenian (Volhynian) Metrica of 1569–1673. Studies on the History of Ukrainian Regionalism in the Polish-Lithuanian Commonwealth*). Ostrog–Lwiv 2002.

Kuliński, Bohdan Andrzej. *Okręt Jego Królewskiej Mości Zygmunta Augusta. Historia galeonu, który nie był galeonem*. Warszawa: Warszawska Firma Wydawnicza, 2012.

Labuda, Gerard. *Źródła, sagi i legendy do najdawniejszych dziejów Polski*. Warszawa: Państwowe Wydawnictwo Naukowe, 1961.

Langer, Andrea. "Die Hirschberger Gnadenkirche 'Zum Kreuze Christi' im künstlerischen Spannungsfeld von Nordeuropäisch geprägtem Protoklassizismus und römisch geprägtem Barock." In *Po obu stronach Bałtyku. Wzajemne relacje między Skandynawią a Europą Środkową. On the Opposite Sides of the Baltic Sea. Relations between Scandinavian and Central European Countries*, edited by Jan Harasimowicz, Piotr Oszczanowski and Marcin Wisłocki, vol. 1, 203–215. Wrocław: Wydawnictwo "Via Nova," 2006.

Lindberg, Bo. "Samuel von Pufendorf." In *Svenskt Biografiskt Lexikon*, vol. 29, ed. Göran Nilzén, 512–522. Stockholm 1995–1997.

Linnarsson, Magnus. "The Development of Swedish Post Office." In *Connecting the Baltic Area. The Swedish Postal System in the Seventeenth Century*, edited by Heiko Droste, 25–47. Stockholm: Södertorns högskola, 2011.

Lipoński, Wojciech. *Narodziny cywilizacji Wysp Brytyjskich*. Poznań: Bene Nati, 1995.

Litwin, Henryk. "Głos w dyskusji." In *Polska na tle Europy XVI–XVII wieku. Konferencja Muzeum Historii Polski 23–24 października 2006*, 109. Warszawa: Muzeum Historii Polski 2007.

Lulewicz, Henryk, and Andrzej Rachuba. *Urzędnicy centralni i dostojnicy Wielkiego Księstwa Litewskiego XIV–XVIII wieku. Spisy.* Kórnik: Biblioteka Kórnicka, 1994.

Lund, Erik A. "The Generation of 1683. The Scientific Revolution and Generalship in the Habsburg Army, 1686–1723." In *Warfare in Eastern Europe, 1500–1800*, edited by Brian L. Davies, 199–248. Leiden–Boston: Brill, 2012.

Löfstrand, Elisabeth, and Laila Nordquist. *Accounts of an Occupied City. Catalogue of the Novgorod Occupation Archives 1611–1617*, vol. 1. Stockholm: Riksarkivet 2005. Skrifter utgivna av Riksarkivet, part 24.

Łopatecki, Karol. "Między włoską a holenderską sztuką fortyfikacyjną. Plan rozbudowy Brześcia Litewskiego w świetle 'Geometrich Plan der Statt Brzesche in Littawen' z 1657 roku." *Zapiski Historyczne*, vol. 74, part 4 (2009): 77–94.

———. "Fortyfikacje Brześcia Litewskiego w dobie II wojny północnej." *Studia i Materiały do Historii Wojskowości*, vol. 43 (2007): 159–176.

———. "Prace kartograficzne wykonane na ziemiach Rzeczypospolitej przez szwedzkich inżynierów wojskowych w XVII stuleciu." *Studia i Materiały do Historii Wojskowości*, vol. 46 (2009): 55–80.

Łygaś, Wojciech. *Szwedzkie opowieści. Z dziejów polsko-szwedzkich XIV–XVIII w.* Gdańsk: Finna, 2005.

Magnusson, Börje. *Att illustrera fäderneslandet – en studie i Erik Dahlberghs verksamhet som tecknare.* Uppsala 1986. Acta Universitatis Upsaliensis, Ars Suetica 10.

Majewski, Andrzej A. "Szarża husarska pod Warszawą 29 lipca 1656 roku." *Przegląd Historyczno-Wojskowy*, no. 241 (2012): 167–174.

Majewski, Wiesław. "Wojna polsko-szwedzka 1655–1660 (potop)." In *Polskie tradycje wojskowe*, part 1, edited by Janusz Sikorski, 296–361. Warszawa: Wydawnictwo Ministerstwa Obrony Narodowej, 1990.

———. "Sienkiewicz – przodek nas, historyków." In *Epoka* Ogniem i mieczem *we współczesnych badaniach historycznych. Zbiór studiów*, edited by Mirosław Nagielski, 85–104. Warszawa: Wydawnictwo DiG, 2000.

Markowicz, Marcin. *Najazd Rakoczego na Polskę.* Zabrze: Inforteditions, 2011.

Maroń, Jerzy. *Wokół teorii rewolucji militarnej. Wybrane problemy (Around the Theory of Military Revolution. Selected Issues).* Wrocław: Wydawnictwo Uniwersytetu Wrocławskiego, 2011.

Matelski, Dariusz. "Straty polskich dóbr kultury w wojnach ze Szwecją w XVII i XVIII wieku oraz próby ich restytucji" (Losses of Polish Cultural Goods during the Swedish Wars in the 17th and 18th Centuries and Restitution Attempts). *Archeion*, vol. 56 (2003): 118–138.

Mączyński, Ryszard M. "Zarys dziejów badań nad zabytkami Warszawy." In *Katalog Zabytków Sztuki. Miasto Warszawa*, part 1: *Stare Miasto*, edited by Jerzy Z. Łoziński, Andrzej Rottermund, 1–35. Warszawa: Wydawnictwa Artystyczne i Filmowe, 1993.

"Medeltiden. Kungl. Maj:ts kansli, Utrikesförvaltningen," edited by Cavaille James and Lindroth Jan, *Riksarkivet beståndsöversikt*, Del 1, Band 2, Stockholm, 1996. Skrifter utgivna av Svenska Riksarkivet 8.

Mosier, John. *The Blitzkrieg Myth. How Hitler and the Allies Misread the Strategic Realities of World War II*. New York: Perennial, 2004.

Nagielski, Mirosław. *Warszawa 1656*. Warszawa: Bellona SA, 2009.

Niléhn, Lars. "On the Use of Natural Law. Samuel Pufendorf as Royal Swedish State Historian". In *Skrifter utgivna av Institutet för rättshistorisk forskning. Rättshistoriska Studier*, vol. 12, 52–69, Stockholm 1986.

Novaky, György. *Handelskompanier och kompanihandel: Svenska Afrikakompaniet 1649–1663: en studie i feodal handel*. Uppsala: Almquist & Wiksell, 1990. Studia Historica Upsaliensia 159.

Nowak, Tadeusz. "Operacja krakowska 1655." In *Wojna polsko-szwedzka 1655–1660*, edited by Jan Wimmer, 207–258. Warszawa: Wydawnictwo Ministerstwa Obrony Narodowej, 1973.

Nowakowski, Paweł. *Iłża. Miasto kościelne*. Radom: Neoflam, 2012.

Olofsson, Sven Ingemar. *Efter Westfaliska Freden. Sveriges yttre politik 1650–1654*. Stockholm: Kungl. Vitterhets Historie och Antikvitets Akademiska handlingar, 1957). Historiska Serien 4.

Olszewski, Henryk, "Myśli o państwie Samuela Pufendorfa." In *Władza i społeczeństwo. Prace ofiarowane Antoniemu Mączakowi w sześćdziesiątą rocznicę urodzin*, edited by Marcin Kamler, Adam Manikowski, Henryk Samsonowicz and Andrzej Wyrobisz, 116–135. Warszawa: Państwowe Wydawnictwo Naukowe, 1989.

Oszczanowski, Piotr. "'Szwedzka sień' we Wrocławiu, czyli 'dyskretna' apoteoza Gustawa II Adolfa" ("'The Swedish Hall' in Wrocław: 'Discreet' Apotheosis of Gustav II Adolph"). In *Po obu stronach Bałtyku. Wzajemne relacje między Skandynawią a Europą Środkową. On the Opposite Sides of the Baltic Sea. Relations between Scandinavian and Central European Countries*, edited by Jan Harasimowicz, Piotr Oszczanowski and Marcin Wisłocki, vol. 1, 69–85. Wrocław: Wydawnictwo "Via Nova," 2006.

Ostapchuk, Victor. "Crimean Tatar Long-Range Campaigns: The View from Remmal Khoja's History of Sahib Gerey Khan." In *Warfare in Eastern Europe, 1500–1800*, edited by Brian L. Davies. Leiden–Boston: Brill, 2012, 147–171.

Pastorek, Anna. "Organizacja floty wojennej Republiki Zjednoczonych Prowincji w XVII wieku. Admiralicje, korpus oficerski, załogi." In *Organizacja armii w nowożytnej Europie. Struktura – urzędy – prawo – finanse*, edited by Karol Łopatecki, 299–311. Zabrze: Inforteditions, 2011.

Pater, Józef. "Kościoły pokoju i łaski przejawem tolerancji religijnej na Śląsku" ("The Churches of Peace and Grace – a manifestation of religious tolerance in Silesia"). In *Religia i polityka. Kwestie wyznaniowe i konflikty polityczne w Europie w XVIII wieku. (Religion and Politics. Religious Issues and Political Conflicts* *in Europe in the 18th Century. On the 300th Anniversary of the Treaty of Altranstädt)*, edited by Lucyna Harc and Gabriela Wąs, 151–154. Wrocław: Wydawnictwo Uniwersytetu Wrocławskiego, 2009.

Perrault, Gilles. *Le Secret du Roi. Premiére partie: La passion polonaise*. Paris: Fayard, 1992.

Polska w okresie drugiej wojny północnej 1655–1660, vol. 3. Edited by Adam Przyboś. Warszawa: Państwowe Wydawnictwo Naukowe, 1957.

Pomian, Krzysztof. *Przeszłość jako przedmiot wiedzy*. Warszawa: Wydawnictwa Uniwersytetu Warszawskiego, 2010.

Reill, Peter Hanns. *The German Enlightenment and the Rise of Historicism*. Berkeley: University of California Press, 1975.

Riese, August. *Die dreitägige Schlacht bei Warschau 28., 29. und 30 Juli 1656*. Breslau 1870.

Roberts, Michael. *Gustavus Adolphus. A History of Sweden 1611–1632*, vol. 1–2. Edinburgh: Longmans, Green & Co., 1957.

———. *The Early Vasas. A History of Sweden, 1523–1611*. Cambridge: Cambridge University Press, 1968.

Rodger, Nicholas Andrew Martin. *The Command of the Ocean. A Naval History of Britain 1649–1815*. London: Penguin Books in association with the National Maritime Museum, 2004.

Sahanovich, Henadz. *Neviadomaia Vaina 1654–1667*. Minsk: Navuka i tekhnika, 1995.

Sauter, Wiesław. *Krzysztof Żegocki, pierwszy partyzant Rzeczypospolitej 1618–1673*. Poznań: Wydawnictwo Poznańskie, 1981.

Schama, Simon. *Landscape and Memory*. New York: Vintage Books, 1995.

Šiaučiūnaitė-Verbickienė, Jurgita. "Tatarzy." In *Kultura Wielkiego Księstwa Litewskiego, analizy i obrazy*, translated by Beata Piasecka, 760–771. Kraków: Universitas, 2011.

Sienkiewicz, Henryk. *The Deluge*, translated by J. Curtin. Boston: Little, Brown and Company, 1915.

Sikora, Radosław. *Fenomen husarii*. Warszawa: Instytut Wydawniczy "Erica," 2013.

Simek, Rudolf. *Mittelerde. Tolkien und die germanische Mythologie*. München: Verlag C.H. Beck, 2005.

Sito, Jakub. "Dahlbergh i inni. O szwedzkich rysownikach – weducistach doby wojennej w Polsce i ich dziele." In *Po obu stronach Bałtyku. Wzajemne relacje między Skandynawią a Europą Środkową. On the Opposite Sides of the Baltic Sea. Relations between Scandinavian and Central European Countries*, edited by Jan Harasimowicz, Piotr Oszczanowski, Marcin Wisłocki, vol. 2, 511–521. Wrocław, Wydawnictwo "Via Nova," 2006.

Skrok, Zdzisław. "Zapomniani świadkowie szwedzkich odwiedzin." *Spotkania z zabytkami*, no. 220 (2005): 5–8.

————. *Wielkie Rozdroże. Ćwiczenia terenowe z archeologii wyobraźni*. Warszawa: Wydawnictwo "Iskry," 2008.

Skworoda, Paweł. *Warka–Gniezno 1656*. Warszawa, Dom Wydawniczy "Bellona," 2003.

Stade, Arne. *Erik Dahlbergh och Carl X Gustafs krigshistoria. Carl Gustaf Studier*, vol. 3. Kristianstad: Militärhistoriska förlaget, 1967.

————. "Geneza decyzji Karola X Gustawa o wojnie z Polską w 1655 r." *Studia i Materiały do Historii Wojskowości*, vol. 19, part 2 (1973): 19–90.

Stahr, Maria. *Medale Wazów w Polsce, 1587–1668*. Wrocław, Zakład Narodowy im. Ossolińskich, 1990.

Stankiewicz, Jerzy. "Ze studiów nad fortyfikacjami pruskimi na ziemiach polskich." *Studia i Materiały do Historii Wojskowości*, vol. 12, part 1 (1966): 106–184.

————. "System fortyfikacyjny Gdańska i okolicy w czasie wojny 1655–1660 r." *Studia i Materiały do Historii Wojskowości*, vol. 20 (1976): 73–121.

————. "Przemiany przestrzenne i demograficzne Gdańska." In *Historia Gdańska*, edited by Edmund Cieślak, vol. 3, 7–35. Gdańsk: Instytut Historii Polskiej Akademii Nauk, Zakład Historii Gdańska i Dziejów Morskich Polski, 1993.

Sułkowska-Kurasiowa, Irena, and Maria Woźniakowa. *Inwentarz Metryki Koronnej. Księgi wpisów i dekretów polskiej kancelarii królewskiej z lat 1447–1795*. Warszawa: Państwowe Wydawnictwo Naukowe, 1975.

Szymański, Józef. *Przewodnik po Wojniczu inaczej*, Wojnicz: Towarzystwo Przyjaciół Ziemi Wojnickiej, 2010.

Taylor, Alan. *American Colonies. The Settling of North America*. London: Penguin, 2001.

Teodorczyk, Jerzy. "Wyprawa zimowa Czarnieckiego w 1656 r." In *Wojna polsko-szwedzka 1655–1660*, edited by Jan Wimmer, 259–295. Warszawa: Wydawnictwo Ministerstwa Obrony Narodowej, 1973.

Tersmeden, Lars. "Carl X Gustafs armé. En konturteckning mot bakgrund av kriget mot Polen." In *Carl X Gustafs armé. Carl – Gustaf Studier*, vol. 8, edited by Arne Stade, 9–47. Kristianstad: Militärhistoriska förlaget, 1979.

————. "Carl X Gustafs armé 1654–1657. Styrka och dislocation". In *Carl X Gustafs armé, Carl – Gustaf Studier*, vol. 8, edited by Arne Stade, 163–276. Kristianstad: Militärhistoriska förlaget, 1979.

Tyszkiewicz, Jan. *Tatarzy w Polsce i Europie. Fragmenty dziejów*. Pułtusk: Akademia Humanistyczna im. A. Gieysztora, 2008.

Tyszkiewicz, Jan. "Krajobraz widziany przez historyka." *Krajobrazy Dziedzictwa Narodowego*, no. 1 (2000): 3–6.

Uddgren, Hugo E. "Rutger von Ascheberg." In *Svenskt Biografiskt Lexikon*, vol. 2, 331–344. Stockhom: Albert Bonniers Förlag, 1920.

Walde, Otto. *Storhetstidens litterära krigsbyten*, vol. 1–2. Stockholm: Almqvist och Wiksells Boktryk, 1916–20.

Wasilkowska, Anna, *Husaria. The Winged Horsemen*. Warszawa: Interpress, 1998.

Widenberg, Johanna. *Fäderneslandets antikviteter. Etniterritoriella historie bruk och integrationssträvanden i den svenska statsmaktens antikvariska verksamhet ca 1600–1720.* Uppsala 2006. Studia Historica Upsaliensia 225.

Wimmer, Jan. "Materiały do zagadnienia liczebności i organizacji armii koronnej w latach 1655–1660." *Studia i Materiały do Historii Wojskowości*, no. 4 (1958): 490–533.

———. "Przegląd operacji 1655–1660." In *Wojna polsko-szwedzka 1655–1660*, edited by Jan Wimmer, 127–206. Warszawa: Wydawnictwo Ministerstwa Obrony Narodowej, 1973.

Włodarski, Józef, and Roman Makutonowicz. "Wywiadowcza penetracja Prus Królewskich i Korony przez Szwedów w latach 1652–1655." In *Komunikacja i komunikowanie w dawnej Polsce*, edited by Krzysztof Stępnik and Maciej Rajewski, 83–94. Lublin: Wydawnictwo Uniwersytetu Marii Curie-Skłodowskiej, 2008.

Wojtasik, Janusz. "Wojna szarpana Stefana Czarnieckiego w dobie potopu szwedzkiego (1655–1660)." In *Z dziejów stosunków Rzeczypospolitej Obojga Narodów ze Szwecją w XVII wieku*, edited by Mirosław Nagielski, 183–200. Warszawa: Wydawnictwo DiG, 2007.

Wolke, Lars Ericson. *1658 Tåget över Bält*. Lund: Historiska Media, 2008.

Wójcik, Zbigniew. "Tło historyczne obrony Klasztoru Jasnogórskiego w roku 1655." In *Częstochowa. Dzieje miasta i Klasztoru Jasnogórskiego*, vol. 1, edited by Feliks Kiryk, 303–335. Częstochowa: Urząd Miasta Częstochowa, 2002.

Wyrozumski, Jerzy. *Dzieje Krakowa. Kraków do schyłku wieków średnich*, vol. 1. Kraków: Wydawnictwo Literackie, 1992.

Ziemierski, Maciej. "Widok szwedzkiego oblężenia Krakowa w 1655 r. autorstwa Erika Jönssona Dahlbergha, kwestie interpretacji." *Krzysztofory*, vol. 22 (2004): 37–41.

Żygulski jun., Zdzisław. *Husaria Polska*. Warszawa: Wydawnictwo "Pagina," 2000.

Internet Resources

Archeowieści. Z pasją o przeszłości:
Wojciech Pastuszka. *O zamku w Gołańczy i masowej mogile z czasów szwedzkiego potopu raz jeszcze.* http://archeowiesci.pl/2010/09/21/o-zamku-w-golanczy-i--masowej-mogile-z-czasow-potopu-raz-jeszcze/ [4 June 2014].

Digital Library of Polish and Poland-Related News Pamphlets from the 16th to the 18th Century:
1. *Brief Pertinentelyck verhalende de effective Conjunctie van den Koningh van Sweeden Met den Kevr – Forst van Brandenburg Mitsgaders de Omstandicheden van het schrickelyk gevecht tusschen de selfde, ende de Polen, vorgevallen den 28.29 ende 30. Julii laestleden. Waer van de Victorie gebleven is by de voorschreve Protestante Princen. Geschreven uyt Warsaw den 4. Augusti. S'graven – Hage, by Adrian Vlacq MDCLVI.* http://cbdu.id.uw.edu.pl/5370/ [4 June 2014].

2. *Kurtzer Bericht der Unmenschlichen Tyranney/ welche der Starosta Babymojsky mit Zuziehung deren in Schlesien sich auffhaltenden Polnischen Edel-Leuten bey nachtlichem Einfall in Welvn/ an der darinnen gelegenen schwedischen Besatzung/ und etzlichen Deutschen graussamster massen von dem 7. Januarii dieses 1656 Jahres biss auf den 12. verübt hat.* http://cbdu.id.uw.edu.pl/6060/1/Z606.djvu [4 June 2014]

Leibniz – Institut für Europäische Geschichte Mainz, database IEG – Friedensverträge:

http://www.ieg-mainz.de/friedensvertraege [4 June 2014].

Kungliga Biblioteket Stockholm:

Magdalena Gram, *Historien om Suecia...* http://www.kb.se/samlingarna/oversikt/suecia/historien-om-sucecia/ [4 June 2014]

The Stanford Encyclopedia of Philosophy:

Seidler, Michael. "Pufendorf's Moral and Political Philosophy." In *The Stanford Encyclopedia of Philosophy* (Spring 2013 Edition), edited by Edward N. Zalta. URL = http://plato.stanford.edu/entries/pufendorf-moral/ [4 June 2014].

University of Warsaw, news:

Kowalski Hubert, and Justyna Jasiewicz. "XVII-wieczne marmury. Skarby z dna Wisły." *Uniwersytet Warszawski. Pismo Uczelni*, no. 56 (February 2012): 30–31. http://portal.uw.edu.pl/c/document_library/get_file?uuid=750ea1a4-72ff-418b-aab3-c9d49a5765ba&groupId=5799051 [7 June 2014].

INDEX[1]

---

[1] Since King Charles X Gustav and Samuel Pufendorf occur on almost every page, these names were omitted in the index.

TECHNICAL EDITOR
Jadwiga Makowiec

PROOFREADER
Justyna Fenrych
Joanna Szczepańska-Włoch
Małgorzata Szul

TYPESETTER
Katarzyna Mróz-Jaskuła

Jagiellonian University Press
Editorial Offices: Michałowskiego St. 9/2, 31-126 Cracow
Phone: +48 12 663 23 81, +48 12 663 23 82, Fax: +48 12 663 23 83